Letts

Whiteboard Activities for Literacy

Leo Sietniekas

Published by Letts Educational
The Chiswick Centre
414 Chiswick High Road
London W4 5TF
Telephone: 020 8996 3333
Fax: 020 8742 8390
E-mail: mail@lettsed.co.uk
Website: www.letts-education.com

Letts Educational is part of the Granada Learning Group.
Granada Learning is a division of Granada plc.

First published 2003

ISBN 1844190404

British Library Cataloguing in Publication Data
A catalogue record for this book is available from the British Library.

This book was designed and produced for Letts Educational by Ken Vail Graphic Design, Cambridge

Commissioned by Kate Newport

Project management by Kate Newport

Edited by Jo Kemp

Illustrations by Liz Bryan

Production by PDQ

Printed and bound in the UK by Ashford Colour Press

Safety notice

Whilst Letts has made all reasonable enquiries to ensure all the third party websites listed in this publication are suitable for KS2 students, Letts Educational does not endorse or approve the content of any such third party websites nor does it accept responsibility or liability for their content. Further, Letts makes no warranty or representation about anything contained in such third party websites referred to herein nor that their URLs will continue to be maintained, available and accessible and accepts no liability in connection with any suggestion or claim that any such third party website breaches any law or regulation or in any other way infringes on any of your rights. Also, you acknowledge that internet sites can change very quickly and Letts Educational accepts no responsibility or liability for any subsequent changes to the contents of any such third party websites, their URLs and/or any other online material.

Letts Educational strongly advises teachers, parents and/or guardians to access, review and monitor all such third party websites before directing students to them and also generally for schools actively to encourage parental supervision of students who are accessing the internet at home.

For government guidance on internet safety in schools, please see:

safety.ngfl.gov.uk/schools

For government advice on internet safety for parents, please see:

safety.ngfl.gov.uk/parents

Contents

Using your Interactive Whiteboard in literacy lessons

Introduction

This book is essentially a huge bank of ideas, linked directly to the National Primary Strategy (NPS), for use with an Interactive Whiteboard (IWB). It does not provide lesson plans, but ideas and starting points for you, the teacher, to use with an IWB to support your literacy lessons. If you are expecting a whole host of finished resources you may be disappointed, for the purpose of this book is to give you generic ideas in the format of the NPS. From there it is hoped that you will create your own resources. My view is that you need the ideas as a starting point and the resources can come later.

Throughout the book the ideas are referenced for use on a Promethean or SMART board, but most are generic to all boards, and so should appeal to all users, regardless of which make of board they use. Some of the ideas are very simple, but they are all linked directly to NLS objectives. Many of the ideas can be modelled by the teacher and then attempted by the students. At Key Stage 1, many of the flipcharts or notebook files for phonics work should be short and simple, to achieve quickly the NLS objective using the medium of the IWB. In Years 4, 5 and 6, an ideal (not always achievable) is to have computers available for groups of children, so that you can set work for them to word-process. This can be saved to disk and then loaded onto the machine controlling the IWB, so that ideas can be presented on the big screen and then altered and discussed. This is a cooperative learning style suited to literacy.

The main idea in using an Interactive Whiteboard is to present information, usually by displaying text or images on screen. This information can be scanned, copied from the Internet (be aware of copyright), or created in Word, Textease/Granada Writer or on a flipchart or notebook page. Information can also be displayed by using commercial software (e.g. a talking book, a reference CD-ROM, or a website like Grid Club) that is fitted into learning objectives and then annotated over (see Figure 1).

Once the information is displayed, children can come up to the board to select text, images or objects and move them around. This is the **key** to using an IWB, as using the select tool well builds participation. In order to engage *all* children when questioning, not just the child who comes out to the board, each child could have a dry wipe board to write on. If your board has infrared connectivity (e.g. a Promethean board), then you can use a slate to control your IWB from anywhere in the room, or let children do this. Wireless technology, such as mice and keyboards, can also be useful here. They can help to maintain the pace of the lesson because children don't have to come out to the board.

Figure 1

Finally, in the independent work part of literacy lessons, you could ask a group of children to work together at an IWB, collaborating on a given task. If you are lucky enough to have the use of computers, then any work created by other groups can be saved and loaded onto the machine running the IWB, so that all work can be displayed. (If you have a network and the relevant software, you can display work from chosen work stations.) If you don't have access to computers, explore the possibility of setting an ICT homework task to be presented at a later date. Try to follow this format for all the tasks you set, to maximise the use of your IWB in supporting literacy. I may not mention this for every point that I cover, but you should try to apply it as often as you can (depending on the pupils' ages and abilities, of course).

Using this book

This book outlines specific ideas for using an IWB with each year group. You will need to use this resource alongside your NLS (National Literacy Strategy) handbook as, wherever possible, I have numbered the ideas to correspond to the right term and section of the NLS. In some cases, objectives have been repeated from previous terms or years, as the NLS requires that previous work be recapped, and I have omitted reference to these, to prevent repetition of the same ideas.

Also, there are other objectives that I have not commented on because they are not appropriate for use with an IWB, so you might notice that the occasional number has been omitted. This could mean that you may encounter numbers 1, 2, 4, 6, etc.

Before we go on to look at the ideas for each year group, I'd like to outline a more detailed overview of techniques that can be used across all key stages.

Presentational use of Interactive Whiteboards

Presentational mode is when you, as a teacher, present information to the class. The pupils observe you and absorb information passively. This kind of activity sets the scene for your lesson and gives the pupils a visual experience on which to base their learning. If you are an inexperienced user of an IWB, this is a good way to start off, and some ideas for activities are given below.

- Showing a video on the screen is very simple and very effective. Larger groups of children can view information in this way.
- Showing PowerPoint presentations is very good, especially when you control the slides using a wireless mouse, for example. You can move around your audience and interact with them – you do not have to be at the front of the class all the time.
- Presenting pictures or slides to elicit response and discussion via IWB software is also powerful, as the images can be sequenced and, moreover, PowerPoint need not be used.
- Logging on to the Internet and viewing a website is another effective way of presenting information/resources.
- Presenting text and simply reading it and asking questions about it is also very powerful.
- CD-ROMs can be a very effective stimulus. There is, indeed, a strong argument that using existing software that has built-in interactivity (e.g. *Wellington Square* or *My World* by Granada Learning) is an efficient and time-saving way to work with an IWB.

So far, I have only mentioned presenting information on a board, rather than writing on one. Within the bullet points above there is a whole host of ideas for presentation. It is important to acknowledge the power that an IWB has to focus attention and motivate, even at presentational level.

Participative use of Interactive Whiteboards

Passive learning via presentation has its place in the learning cycle, but retention and development of knowledge are improved when pupils **participate** in the lesson. You don't need to be an expert IWB user to engage your pupils in this mode of learning. Even if you feel a little overawed by new technology, you can get started with an IWB by treating the board as a big computer screen, and using a pen or finger as a mouse. Simply click on the screen to move pages or activities. If you can do this on a computer screen then you can do it on a larger version!

Pupils must be encouraged to come forward and use the IWB. In this way, they become *active* learners rather than *passive* learners. This happens very simply. All they need to know is how to use the **select**, **pen**, **highlight** and **rub out** tools – the ICT does not get in the way.

Ideas for participation

- 'Chalk and talk' can be done with an IWB simply by using the pen and rub out tools to write on the board and then rub things out. This is something we do regularly in our teaching, but it can lead to passive learning by the children – we write, they listen. With an IWB, however, children can participate and become active learners by doing the writing themselves – and we listen!

- Write notes about a discussion – the children make suggestions and you scribe the text. (Children, if able, could also scribe the text.)
- Change the colour of text to indicate a part of a sentence. Ask the children which part of the text you are referring to.
- Make text larger or smaller.
- Highlight your text to show a part of speech. Ask a child to do the same thing.
- Model writing, then ask the children to come out and write on a new page or over prepared text.
- Create flow diagrams in order to 'brainstorm' an idea. If possible, get the children to write the ideas on the board.
- Draw simple pictures and label them. Encourage your children to come out to the IWB as much as possible.

Using your Interactive Whiteboard in literacy lessons

- Draw pictures in or out of sequence. Use the select tool and ask the children to rearrange them.
- Write out words in halves and then join them together. Get the children to use the select tool to do the joining.
- Write words with missing syllables or prefixes and get the children to join them together using the select tool.
- Write out sentences with missing capital letters and ask the children to correct them.
- Write out sentences with punctuation errors and ask the children to correct them. The variety here is almost endless.
- Write out sentences that have grammatical errors and ask the children to come to the board to correct them. Again, the variety here is huge.
- Highlight verbs (you model the work), then get the children to do it.
- Highlight nouns (you model the work), then get the children to do it.
- Draw pictures and create captions. Get the children to make suggestions. Eventually ask the children to do it themselves.
- Indulge in 'cloze procedure' on a subject of your choice (not just literacy). The children can fill in the spaces or drag correct answers from a given list.
- Show letter formation on a large scale (handwriting). You can model handwriting techniques and then ask the children to emulate you. Most boards (e.g. SMART, Promethean and Hitatchi) have lines that you can insert onto pages as templates.
- Create a quick word bank for children to use in oral work.
- Play hangman on screen, but make the vowels red and consonants blue. This means changing pen colours.
- Write out a sentence in the wrong order and get the children to use the select tool to reorder it.
- Save your flipcharts for another day. You have numerous pages on an IWB to play with. This saves you having to wipe the dreaded ordinary whiteboard time and time again.
- Use the marquee select tool to create poetry from pre-written phrases by dragging them into a readable order.

The ideas above can all be implemented using the pen and marker tool, the rub out tool and the select tool. As a fledgling Interactive Whiteboard user, you could be in front of a class in minutes doing literacy lesson introductions that enable your children to participate with you in their learning. The beauty of this is that you won't need your paper flipcharts, which get so messy, because you have a virtually limitless supply of electronic ones. Neither do you need a variety of marker pens, as one does the trick on an IWB, plus you have an endless supply of colours! Also, if you make and error on a normal board it stays, whereas on an IWB you can rub it out or undo it. If you have used big books in the past, you will be amazed at how much more children can see textually in comparison.

As a novice, you will be able to do all these things with very little training or making of special resources. Just tell yourself to do the things electronically that you would normally do with an ordinary marker pen. In addition, you don't need to worry about space – just write a few words on one page and then move to the next.

You will need to be careful about the pace of your lesson, in that children coming out to the board and thinking about what they are going to write or select may slow things down. It is a good idea to use dry wipe boards so that all children work at the same time and are thus all involved.

Here are some more ideas that involve the children participating in the lesson.

- Write out a word freehand, then undo the letters so that you only have one left. Ask the children to spell the word, then reveal it a letter at a time using the redo/undo button. If you join the letters without a break, you can do the same for words to reveal a sentence.
- Use the text tool to print a word, then 'write' over it in thick white pen mode. (Select the pen and then the 'white' colour and write over your printed text. You'll find it disappears.) This covers the text with a white layer which can then be removed by rubbing it out. Use this technique to reveal a sentence (see Figure 2), or write a sentence mixed up all over the board, cover the words or letters in white (ensure you work on a white background) and then play a game of find the word, read it and then put it into a correct sequence using the select tool.

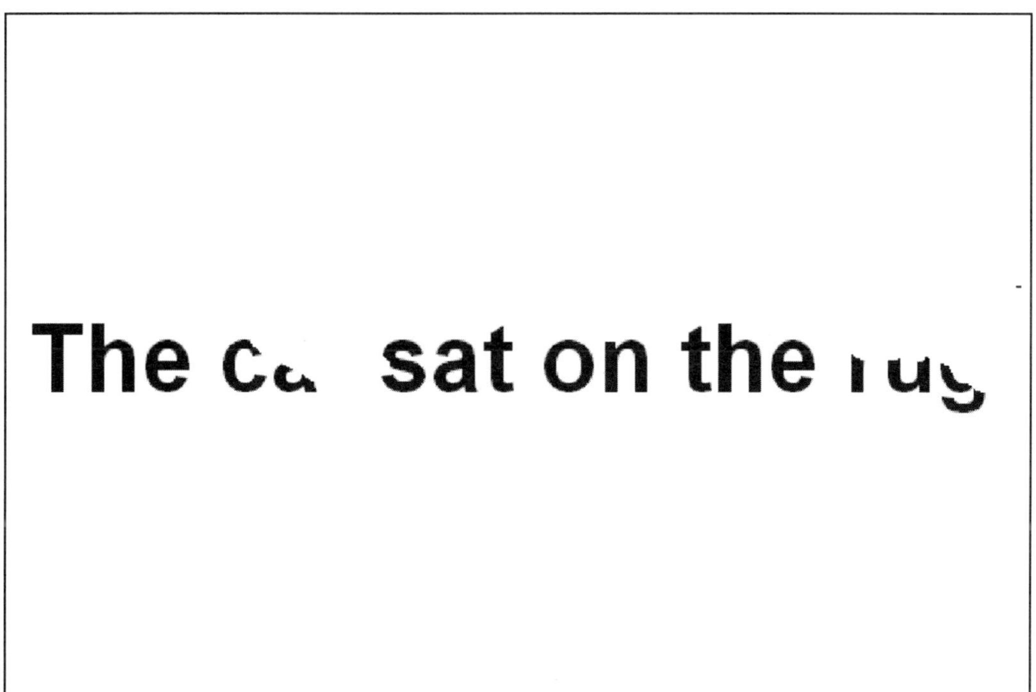

Figure 2

Using your Interactive Whiteboard in literacy lessons

- Write out some sentences or words and use the reveal tool (or curtain tool) to show a little at a time. You could do this for a sequence of pictures to focus the children on one thing at a time.
- Use the spotlight tool to create a focus on a single word or letter. This is great fun and goes down well with the children.
- Is your handwriting too scruffy? Use the character recognition tool to create instant printed text. This can be used to contrast writing and text. The children can use this tool or an on-screen typewriter. Most boards have some form of character recognition.

Participation using other applications

A really powerful feature of all IWBs is that they can control other applications and allow you to annotate or write over them.

- You can type out a poem in unsequenced phrases using, say, Word and insert/paste it onto a flipchart or SMART notebook page phrase by phrase. Then create your own poem by choosing the phrases you want with the select tool. Alternately, you can annotate or write over a poem created in a word processing document.
- Annotate a Word document created in cloze format using the pen. Alternatively, copy and paste the document and annotate it from within the flipchart.
- Create printed text with missing commas, full stops, nouns, etc. Ask the children to fill them in with the pen. This can be done as annotating text in, say, Word or in flipchart mode. Numerous permutations are possible here.
- Develop ideas to create a story. You can use PowerPoint, Word or Publisher and annotate over it, or use an IWB flipchart and then write down ideas on the chart/page. You could make notes on starts, characters, settings, dialogue, endings, etc. More able children could do the scribing.
- You could show text on screen and indulge in literal or inferential comprehension. This could be oral or written on an actual flipchart. Text could be used as a starting point for a discussion. (It could be text in Word or flipchart mode.)
- You can highlight any text in any application and then copy it onto your flipchart. You must paste it into the rich-text box and it will allow you to edit it in flipchart mode. This method works for Promethean boards. If you don't have one, use copy/paste.
- Use a CD-ROM, e.g. a talking book, and annotate it as appropriate. The skill of the teacher in eliciting answers to questions remains intact.
- Connect to the Internet and search for authors, e.g. use **www.google.co.uk**. Read and annotate Internet pages on subjects of genre, or paste sections onto a flipchart/notebook file to analyse and discuss. (NB Be aware of copyright.) Knowledge of an IWB camera tool is very useful here.

- Connect to the Internet and log on to a newspaper site, e.g. **www.thisishull.co.uk**, and annotate as appropriate.
- Use the camera tool to take a snapshot of any text or pictures on your computer and paste it onto your flipchart. You can then annotate your text as you wish.
- Use the camera tool to capture pictures from the Internet or elsewhere and paste them onto your flipchart. If you visit **www.images.google.com**, you can snapshot an almost unlimited range of pictures for your work. The images can then be saved to your image library or an IWB page for use in your literacy lessons as a visual stimulus.
- Design an advert. Insert an image or copy and paste it onto your flipchart and then write slogans using the pen or printed text.
- Write a comic book story. Draw pictures, save them to flipchart, rearrange them using the select tool and then add captions. Alternatively, use a series of inserted digital photographs to create a story sequence and then add captions.
- Colour your text to follow the sequence of traffic lights. Show the introductory part of your paragraph as green – this starts off the sentence. Colour development sentences yellow or orange – this is like motoring along in a car. Colour the concluding sentence red – this is like a stop light at a set of traffic lights. The idea follows the sequence of traffic lights but is linked into creating a paragraph. The children could come out and do this. This is a good exercise for showing how to format a paragraph.
- Children type in text to practise using upper and lower case. This can be done as a class or group activity. They can use an on-screen keyboard for this.
- You can write into a Word document using the on-screen keyboard or the pen with the character recognition tool switched on. This allows you to alter your original document.
- Use any clipart CD-ROM (e.g. the *Oxford Reading Tree Clipart CD-ROM*) to create your own stories on a flipchart, adding links to sounds. This is done very easily on a Promethean or SMART board, but would need the use of PowerPoint or Clicker4 for other boards.
- Insert a picture onto an IWB page and ask the children to create the back-cover blurb for a book (see Figure 3).
- Use the annotations in the annotations library to add drawings quickly to your flipchart. Shapes and arrows would be helpful to assist in developing ideas in literacy. You would use the SMART gallery for adding saved annotations.
- Create a writing frame, or paste one from Word or Microsoft Publisher, and save it as a library page for later use. This can be done using Promethean software. If you have a different board, save it as an IWB chart or file. On a SMART board, this can be done as a template in the SMART gallery.

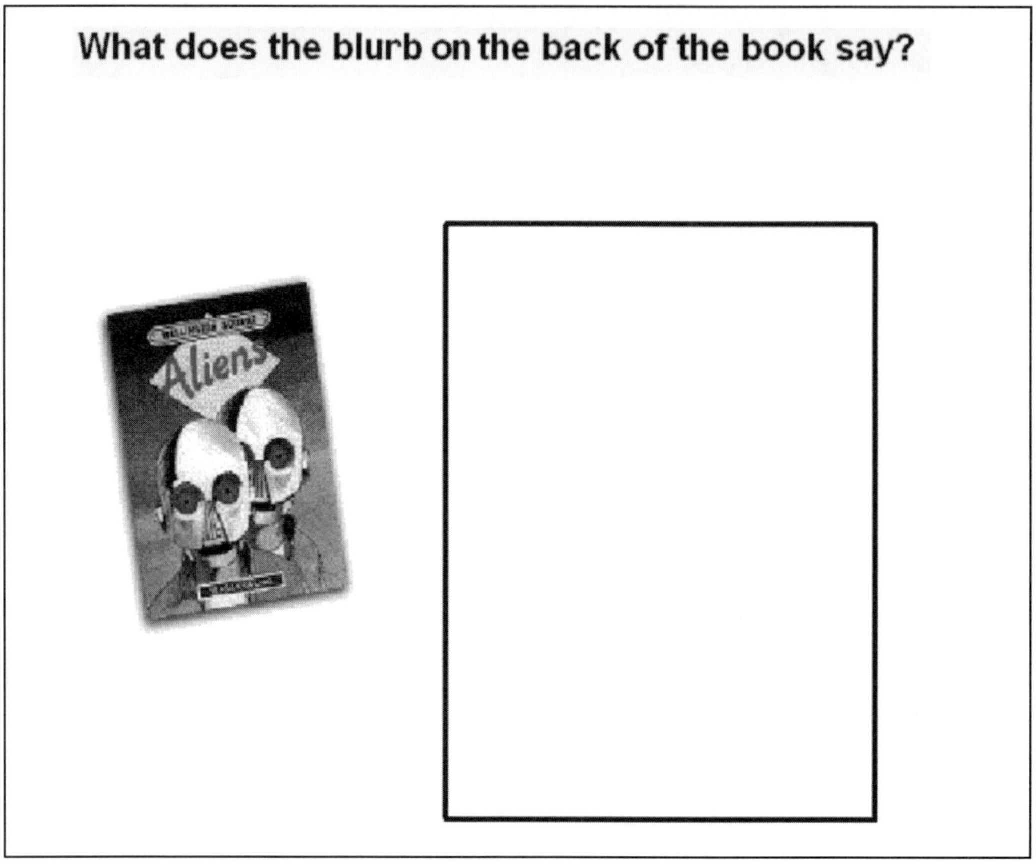

Figure 3

- Use the callouts in the annotations library or SMART template folder to help with the study of dialogue. If you have a different board, you can copy/paste callouts from Word.

Up to now, I have outlined ideas that a user with very little training can apply to their literacy lessons. Most of these ideas are generic to all boards. Hopefully, by now, your children are participating in the lesson by coming out and doing various activities on the board. It is worth mentioning at this point that the skilful use of Granada Writer or Textease (Studio) will allow you to create text or parts of text that can be moved around a screen by clicking on that text to select it and then clicking to allow you to move it. Pictures can be moved in the same way. The Promethean/SMART board has software that allows you to do all the above activities, but Granada Writer/Textease will do a similar job for you.

Progression to interactive use of Interactive Whiteboards —

At this point I'd like to introduce the idea of **interactivity**. How can we get the children to work collaboratively at the board? Think about this and we'll come back to it later. Meanwhile, here are some more ideas that will lead you on to this idea of interactivity.

- Link letters to sounds, so that children can hear them as they touch them with the pen. They'll have to choose the select tool to move them. This is more easily done using Promethean software, but can also be achieved using SMART, Word, PowerPoint or Granada Writer/Textease.

- You can add sounds to individual words, so that children can build up sentences they might find difficult to read by first listening to the words, then selecting them to place them in a sentence.
- Use the page selector tool to create flipcharts with several pages (Promethean software). You could use the thumbnail pages on a SMART board as an alternative, or the page turning arrows.
- Having done that, why not put a verse of a poem on each page for the children to work on? They could even add a new verse on a blank page.
- You could ask the children to create paragraphs of a story, with one on each page. One group at a time could come out in the guided session and work together. (Do I sense a collaborative approach to using the IWB here?)
- Ask the children to create a chapter of a story per page. This would work better with groups working at a board collaborating with each other.
- Ask the children to add an ending or a middle to a poem or a story. This will require inserting a page. On a Promethean board, right-click on a page and select 'insert'. On a SMART board, simply insert a page using the insert button or add page icon. (More collaboration?)
- Write a comic story using drawings on separate pages with children writing the speech. (More collaboration?)
- You and the children can add your own drawings to the annotation library. On a Promethean board, right-click on a drawing and select 'add to annotation library'. (This only works on a Promethean board.)
- With a Promethean board, you can use the clock tool to time spelling tests and turn flipchart pages automatically.
- With a Promethean board, you can use the Tickertape tool to scroll learning objectives across the screen.
- With a Promethean board, you can use the Internet button to connect to the Internet from within a flipchart. Alternatively, open up the Internet normally and annotate. On a SMART board, you can write a web address the same way as in Word and press CTRL click to connect.
- With a Promethean board, you can insert images to help you create flipcharts by clicking on the smiley face icon and inserting an image. Otherwise, insert a picture using the insert button.
- You can copy and paste images from Word or the Internet and use them on a flipchart.
- With a Promethean board, you can save your images to the image library and then use them freely in your teaching. With a SMART board you save them to the SMART gallery. Most board manufacturers are now developing their own versions of resources, but Granada Writer and Textease allow you access to your files across your computer very easily.
- You can use the hyperlinks to create links to anywhere on your computer. This

means you can make a link to sound files to be used in literacy. This has huge implications for inclusion ideas, as children who find it difficult to access text can hear it. This would be very useful when children work at the board for collaborative and interactive learning. Promethean software lets you do this very easily, but it can also be done within Word, PowerPoint and Granada Writer/Textease if you don't have a Promethean board.

- You can make links to video files so that an extract will play in a flipchart at the press of a button. Promethean software lets you do this very easily, but it can also be done within Word, Publisher, PowerPoint and Textease. SMART boards have their own video player, plus you can now hyperlink to a selected video file within SMART notebook.
- The above can also be applied to a music file.
- Use a flipchart to create a shape poem (see Figure 4).

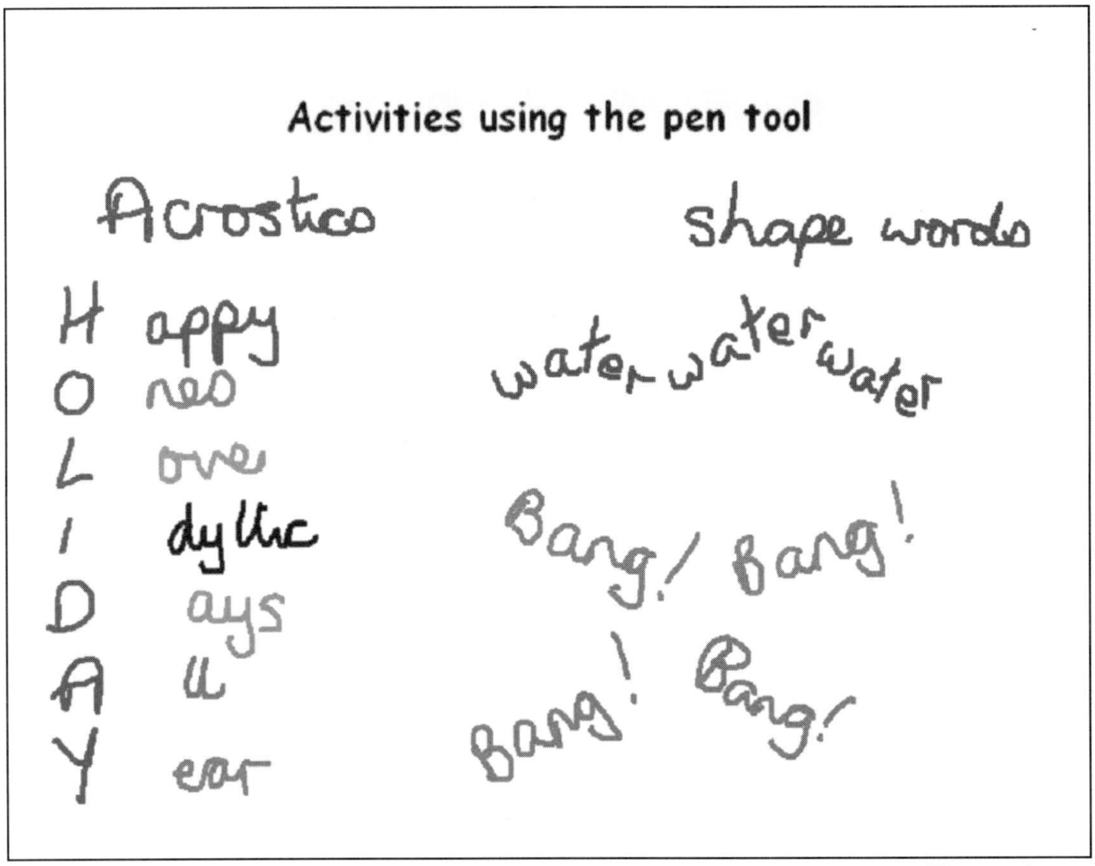

Figure 4

- Use a flipchart to create an acrostic poem (see Figure 4).
- With a Promethean board, you can split the flipchart screen to work on or annotate a piece of software in one half of your desktop, and make notes on your actual flipchart and save it for later. If you don't have a Promethean board, you will have to use the minimise tool.

At The University of Hull, we believe there is a pedagogical argument that collaborative/interactive work on the part of children leads to the best and deepest learning. Using this concept, here is an outline of how I believe an IWB can be used most effectively across literacy lessons, using techniques ranging from presentation to collaboration.

The following is an example idea of the progression to 'interactivity'. You may wish to introduce a chosen text on a chart for the children to listen to and then read with you. This is a passive learning start. The rest of the ideas below are then based on your chosen text.

- You may wish to tell the children about some spelling rule and then illustrate it. You do the modelling, using a flipchart to write on – passive learning to start with.
- The children can come up to the board and join up word halves or highlight phonemes according to your learning objectives. (They are starting to participate in word level work.)
- You may then want to do some sentence level work, say on identifying verbs from the text. The children can come out and highlight relevant words. (Participation, motivation and focused attention.)
- For text level work, you may want to identify aspects of character from text. The text can be displayed on an IWB, along with an image or even a video clip. Children could be asked to split up into groups to discuss this. One group could be asked to come out to the board and write about the character, then report back to the class in the plenary. This is collaboration and deeper learning. Other groups could, if computers were available to each group, write about character, save it to disk, load it onto the computer running the IWB and then display their own findings, too.

I always try to create flipcharts with these three elements in mind, as a kind of progression in the use of an IWB to create different levels of learning.

In summary

- Implications for this approach are that children, as well as teachers, can and should be board users.
- Teachers can use this model of learning when they have built up confidence and skills with the board.
- There is nothing wrong with you presenting work and the children listening, as long as this fits in with your planning and you are aware that the other modes need to be catered for. These can wait until you have built up confidence, but I would suggest you get the children using the board at the earliest opportunity so that they can participate.
- Interactivity need not be a flipchart that has wonderful colour or sound or video. It's how the board gets the children to interact that is important. Time is precious, so if it takes hours of your time to make a flipchart then make simpler resources!

Using your Interactive Whiteboard in literacy lessons

- Make your flipcharts for literacy simple, and try not to put too much text on a flipchart. You could, of course, add a worksheet page at the end to display class tasks, so avoiding lots of photocopying.
- If you are a beginner, try making one literacy flipchart per week or fortnight, but after a term be stricter with yourself and agree to use one as often as possible, even if you simply have to use one for writing on as you would an ordinary board.
- Simply writing on an IWB or running software is a great way to start!
- If you are lucky enough to have an IWB in your class, then it's really your duty to justify its purchase and use it to death. Throw away your old board and use nothing else. Pretty soon you'll want nothing else.
- If you have to share a board, use it as often as possible. Times are busy and hard, but this tool is here to stay and it will ultimately save you time because you can save everything and come back to it later.
- Don't expect instant solutions and flipcharts/notebook files to be made for every occasion. Remember, every teacher alters worksheets to suit them, so the same will happen to flipcharts. Use what is already available to save time.
- Having said this, share your charts because in giving, others will give to you. The Promethean and SMART sites are building such a resource, and other providers will do the same in time.
- This is a new technology, and new resources for it are constantly being made, but the true potential of the boards is yet to be realised. This way of teaching on an IWB is the future and is an ideal way of developing your teaching professionally.

I'm now going to look at the various year groups and outline specific ideas for using the board. I have included, where possible, references to other resource materials, so time is saved in making appropriate flipcharts. There is a list of software at the end of the book, broken down into KS1 and KS2, for you to refer to. As you work from this book, it would be a good idea to have a copy of the NLS handbook to hand, as a cross-reference guide to the numbers within each section – they are interlinked. I have not rewritten the NLS (although it feels like it!) so you will need to refer to both to get the best value.

Word level work

Phonological awareness, phonics and spelling

1 Explore rhyming patterns by writing them on the IWB or using Sherston's *Nursery Rhyme Time* as a CD-ROM source. You can annotate over them and use them as a starting point for your own rhymes. You can sing along or simply read with your pupils. You could generate your own rhymes, with the children making them up and with you acting as scribe. Drawings instead of words could be used. You can use the Clicker4 materials on nursery rhymes to carry out these activities.

2 Write down letters and words on a flipchart and then link them to a sound file. When the children press on a word, it will speak. The words can then be highlighted (hyperlinks need to be turned off) and moved around (Promethean board). The children can also read the letters out loud and come out to the board and write them. You could do this using the insert object command (select wav file) or use Granada Writer or Textease.

- Write the letters of the alphabet on a flipchart/notebook, display them to the class in either handwritten or printed format, and then read them. Ask the children to come to the board and write them as you say them. A SMART board is useful here as fingers instead of pens can be used.
- Read the phonemes a–z, ch, sh and th. Associate them with words written on a flipchart/notebook. Get the children to highlight them using the highlighter tool.
- Identify initial and final phonemes in CVC words by writing them down and getting the children to highlight them on a flipchart/notebook. Use CVC words on flipcharts for recognising initial letters (see Figure 5). Play at joining the initial letters to the rest of the CVC word. Use the select tool for this.

3 Make a flipchart/notebook with lower and upper case letters on separate pages and mix them up. Get the children to use the select tool to put them in alphabetic order. Say the name of a word and a child writes that letter on the flipchart. Granada Writer/Textease or My World for Early Years could be used to achieve this if you want to use pre-prepared software.

4 Use an IWB to help with sound and spelling patterns by:

- selecting families of similar CVC words using the select tool, e.g. 'hop', 'top', 'mop'. Mix them up on a flipchart/notebook and then get the children to match them up.
- writing out words and talk about onsets and rimes. Then get the children to come up to the IWB and say the word and mark an onset or rime with the pen or highlighter tool, e.g. 'tip', 'skip', 'flip', 'chip'.

- creating a list of familiar words on a flipchart/notebook and asking the children to identify the ones with the same letter (alliteration). The children could try to make up their own words.

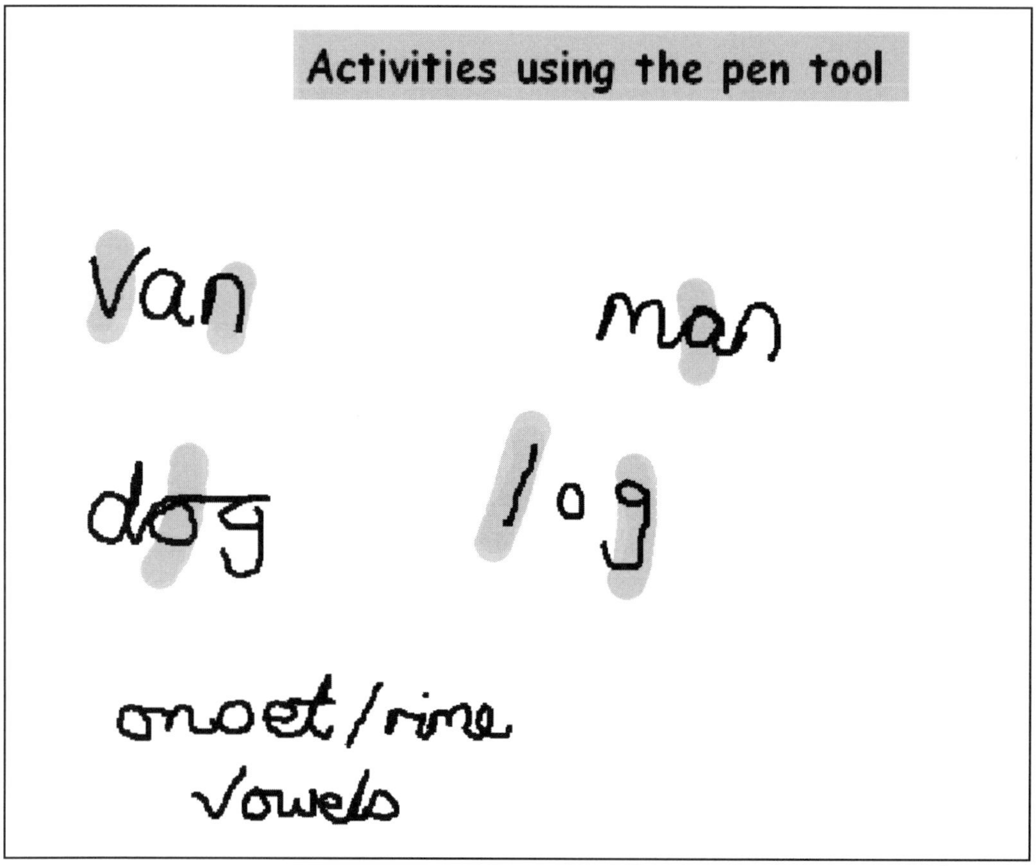

Figure 5

Word recognition, graphic knowledge and spelling

5 Create a list of favourite words and display them on the IWB (possibly linked to sound files) to practise sight vocabulary. Write a selection of the words on another page and re-read the words.

6 Create a list of 45 most common words from Appendix 1 of the NLS handbook (p.60), e.g. ‘I’, ‘up’, ‘look’, ‘we’, etc. You could link these to pictures and sounds. Place them on a flipchart/notebook and use the resource to sight-read the words. A Promethean resource library already contains lots of these lists. Avoid putting all the words on one page as they would make it look cluttered.

7 Use a talking book or other text to practise reading. Ask children what they understood. Control the book and annotate using the IWB software.

8 Invite children to write their own name on the board. Use a tiled background (lined) to help letter orientation.

9 Look at words displayed on the IWB and examine their shape, length and any common spelling patterns. Highlight or mark accordingly.

Handwriting

10 Use a tiled background with handwriting lines to help begin handwriting (grip and controlled line). You could model handwriting on the board. Children could trace letter patterns in the air with their fingers.

Sentence level work

Grammatical awareness

1. Use a talking book displayed on the IWB to make sure the children know that text should make sense. Annotate and control the book, as necessary.
2. During the reading of the talking book or displayed text, invite the children to predict what might happen next. Write on the IWB what they predict.
3. Check that the children are reading from left to right. Get them to come to the board to show which way the text flows. They could use a pen tool to draw an arrow showing direction.
4. Display the children's names on the IWB and get them to write a capital letter over the start of their names. If writing is a challenge, they could begin by tracing over their written name with their fingers, and then a pen.

Text level work

Reading

Understanding print

1. Shared reading carried out by displaying text on the board.
   - Children recognise printed and written work in a variety of printed and handwritten formats. Handwriting could be scanned in and then displayed on a flipchart/notebook. Create a resource of words in the form of labels, signs, letters, notices, lists, directions, adverts, newspaper extracts, etc., and display these on the IWB. Move them around or annotate as appropriate.
   - Create a word bank of correct terms about books and print, e.g. cover, beginning, end, page, line, word, letter, title. Invite the children to come up to the board and show which is which.
   - Use the IWB to track text with the children. Annotate the text appropriately.

Reading comprehension

2. Display text on a flipchart/notebook and begin to point out the structure of the text. Use a pen tool to annotate as you wish.
3. Highlight unfamiliar words. You can use a talking book as a source and display it on the IWB.

4–6 These can rely on displaying the text on the IWB with the teacher and children annotating as appropriate. Number 4 relates to noting the differences between spoken and written forms. Number 5 relates to identifying formal elements of story writing, e.g. 'Once there was'. Number 6 refers to displaying a variety of text via an IWB, so a collection would need to be made.

7 The children could draw any main events on the IWB and speak about them or point to pictures in a story (as displayed on the IWB).

8 Use the highlighter or pen tool to recognise and show phrases and captions from texts.

9 Use text displayed on the IWB to show story structures. Here, you could use the highlighter tool to mark appropriate parts of the text.

10 Display stories and rhymes on the IWB (via the Internet or CD-ROMs, as mentioned at the back of the book) to highlight rhyming patterns.

Writing

Understanding print

11 You can use the IWB to display the following points:

- sending and recording messages
- writing remains constant
- writing and drawings in books are different to a child's own work
- writing is formed one word at a time
- how letters are formed and that they merge to create words
- apply letter/sound correspondences when helping the teacher to model work.

The teacher models the writing using the IWB and encourages the children to come out and write on it (using fingers on a SMART board). This will show the children how writing is formed one word at a time, for example. (Make sure the board is low enough for the children to use.)

Composition

12 Children can do the following activities on the IWB:

- write their names
- write labels or captions for pictures
- write a sentence to match a picture.

  You might like to use 2Simple software or Granada Writer/Textease for this activity. If using the pen tool proves too difficult, then use an on-screen keyboard.

13. A group of children could work at the board and draw/write about what they intend to do – this is collaborative learning. A teacher, classroom support assistant or other classroom helper might be needed to oversee this activity and help the children at the board.
14. A group of children can collectively tell a story based on a previous one they have read.
15. The children could come up to the board to talk about their own experiences. If you can display pictures on the IWB, or even letters and words, the children could use the select tool to move them around the screen. Writing on a big screen is a tricky skill at this age, so moving things around to match them may be preferable. Use a collection of lists, signs, directions, menus, labels, greetings cards and letters.

Children at this age will need help to do these activities, so the use of a teaching assistant to help and encourage them would be very useful. If children don't have the ability to write on the board, then you can do it for them virtually and start to train them to do so.

Year 1

Not every point has been covered because there is a certain amount of revision of content covered in the previous year.

Term 1 Word level work

Phonological awareness, phonics and spelling

1 Explore rhyming patterns by viewing them on the IWB and then annotating and joining groups of patterns together using the select tool, e.g. hat, fat, mat. You can use word lists on a flipchart/notebook or Clicker4.

2 Rearrange letters of the alphabet using the select tool to practise alphabetical letter knowledge and order. My World Literacy for Early Years has an excellent CD-ROM that has screens ready for use which are displayable on the IWB and can be annotated over.

3 Practise working with CVC words by saying the words as displayed on the IWB and then using the pen or highlighter tool to annotate the initial or final phonemes. The CVC words could be grouped together using the select tool. Softease has created a Literacy curriculum resource pack which is full of screens that cover word and sentence level work for KS1. Text and images are movable within the screens and therefore well worth considering for use on an IWB.

4 Create a flipchart/notebook and then add CVC words. Highlight each phoneme using the highlighter tool. You might like to add a space between each letter.

5 Split the CVC words into phonemes and then use the select tool to join or blend them together. Creating these as text means making each letter individually, which can be done using the whiteboard character recognition tool.

6 You can model writing the three phonemes in CVC words by asking the children to spell the word orally, and then to try to write it. The CVC words can be grouped using the select tool. The undo or redo tools could be put to good use here. If you use Textease, you can use a mouse-over function, where you pass a mouse over a word and it disappears for a set amount of time, then reappears. This will give the children time to indulge in look, cover, say and spell.

Word recognition, graphic knowledge and spelling

7 Create a flipchart/notebook of high-frequency words linked to a graded book on an IWB. Carry out matching halves, marking beginnings and ends, matching meanings to words by using the tools of the flipchart (select, pen and highlighter tool). My World, Granada Writer or Textease will carry out the same function.

8 Read on sight other common words as displayed on the IWB. You could use pictures to match to words using the select tool.

9 Make a flipchart containing 30 high-frequency words for Year 1 and Year 2 from NLS handbook Appendix List 1. Annotate and highlight as appropriate.

10 Create a list of words to display on the IWB and highlight lengths of words, any words within words and common spelling patterns. Use several pages for the list in order to avoid cluttering up the screen.

11 Spell common irregular words from Appendix List 1 (p.61 of the NLS handbook) by joining halves together. Use the select tool (see Figure 6).

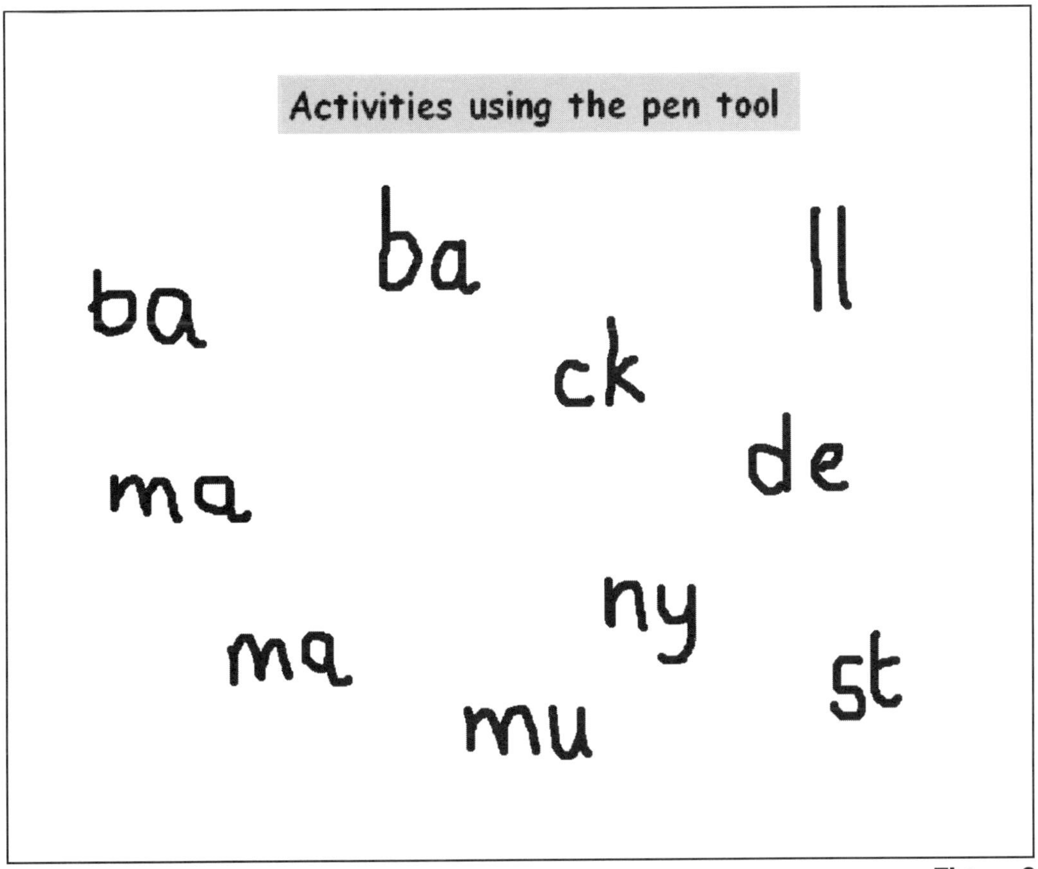

Figure 6

Vocabulary extension

12 On a flipchart/notebook, make lists of new words when they are experienced during the literacy lesson. The children could write them out on the board using character recognition. Save them for revisits.

Handwriting

13 Show the children how to hold an IWB pen.

14 Use the IWB (tiled with lines) to practise lower case writing that can then be joined up.

Term 2 Word level work

Phonological awareness, phonics and spelling

1 Identify letter sounds by joining up the initial, medial and final sounds to the rest of the word. This can be done by using the select tool. Words need to be created by typing in each letter separately so they can be moved using the select tool. (If you write a whole word, you will have to move the word as a whole object and not as individual letters or blends.)

2 Add endings, e.g. 'll', 'ff', 'ss', 'ng' to the rest of a word using the select tool. For example, write 'fa', then use the select tool to join 'll' to it. With a Promethean/SMART board, you could use the rub out tool to reveal the ending of a word by colouring over it with white pen on a white background.

3 Join initial blends, e.g. 'bl', 'cr', 'tr', 'str'. to other word halves using the select tool. For example, 'bl' can be added to 'ack' to make 'black'.

The same method can be used with final blends, e.g. 'nd', 'ip', 'st'. Use the select tool to add these endings to the roots of words. For example, 'st' can be added to 'la' to make 'last'.

Use the highlighter tool to identify phonemes within words. Blend phonemes by using the select tool on the IWB.

Word recognition, graphic knowledge and spelling

4 This involves sight vocabulary work from a saved flipchart/notebook word list. You could link words to pictures using the select tool. A talking book could be used and annotated over.

5 Create a list on the IWB of familiar words to refer to and learn by heart. Save the pages for future revisits.

6 Create another flipchart/notebook with 30 more high-frequency words from NLS handbook Appendix 1 and save it.

7 Display words on the IWB and highlight lengths, common patterns, or words within words.

8 Learn plurals using a flipchart/notebook with singular words on it and add 's' using the select tool. You may need to use the pen tool if spellings change.

9 Spell common irregular words using the curtain tool to act as the cover part in 'look, cover, say, spell'. The children could also spell out the word on the board orally. Alternatively, simply undo the words and get the children to respell them. You could also switch between flipchart or notebook pages.

Vocabulary extension

10 Create a stored word list of words linked to particular topics or shared experiences, and save them on IWB software or annotate over a list created in Word.

Handwriting

11 Practise handwriting using a tiled surface to ensure groups of children get the sizing of their letters correct. Tiled backgrounds can be obtained on Smart, Hitatchi and Promethean boards.

Term 3 Word level work

Phonological awareness, phonics and spelling

1 Use a flipchart/notebook to annotate, select or change the colour of long vowel phonemes, e.g. oo, ai, ie, oa. Create a word list, then highlight relevant vowel phonemes. You could create a short piece of text containing long vowels and then ask the children to highlight or ring them using the pen tool. You could also create a list of words with the long vowel phonemes missing and insert them using the pen or select tool.

Use the words in NLS handbook Appendix List 3 to practise the splitting up of words into their respective phonemes. You could highlight them or simply move them using the select tool to separate them. You would need to create each letter separately if you wanted to use the select tool. This might be time consuming, so highlighting might be an easier option.

Word recognition, graphic knowledge and spelling

2 Create a flipchart/notebook with high-frequency words for sight-reading.

5 Display words with two or three common spelling patterns on the IWB, then show them on another page all jumbled up. Use the select tool to match them up or classify them.

6 Learn spellings ending in 'ed' and 'ing'. Use the flipchart to add the past and present verb endings to the relevant action words. Use the select tool. Write out text and ask the children to change it to the past or present, as appropriate, by the use of annotation.

7 Make a list of the common irregular words from NLS handbook Appendix List 1 and display for annotation and sight-reading. You could match these to images by using the select tool.

Vocabulary extension

8 On a flipchart/notebook, make a list of new words the children have discovered and save it.

9 Sight-read the words 'vowel' and 'consonant'. Use the rub out tool or undo tool to spell (write out the word 'vowel' and press the undo tool until only the v is left; press the reveal tool to show the next letter, etc.). You could also switch to a new page to rewrite the word with the help of the children.

Handwriting

10 Practise handwriting on a tiled surface, paying attention to the size of the letters formed.

Term 1 Sentence level work

Grammatical awareness

1 Read text written on the IWB screen. Check that it makes sense. Annotate as desired.

2 Use grammatical awareness to predict text. Display text on the IWB and invite the children to say what happens next. You can model the answer for them or they can respond orally.

3 Read text with appropriate expression and intonation. Use a talking book or your own typed text. Use the flipchart/notebook tools to control the CD-ROM and annotate appropriately.

4 Write out a caption and re-read to check whether it makes sense. You can act as scribe for the children. Create text with words missing or in the wrong order, and ask the children to spot the omissions or reorder the words using the select tool. You can do this with IWB software or an application like Granada Writer. Remember to create words separately so you can move them about one by one.

Sentence construction and punctuation

5 Write a sentence on the IWB with capital letters and full stops, and get the children to highlight these. Create text with missing or incorrect capital letters and full stops, and get the children to use the pen tool to insert them (see Figure 7).

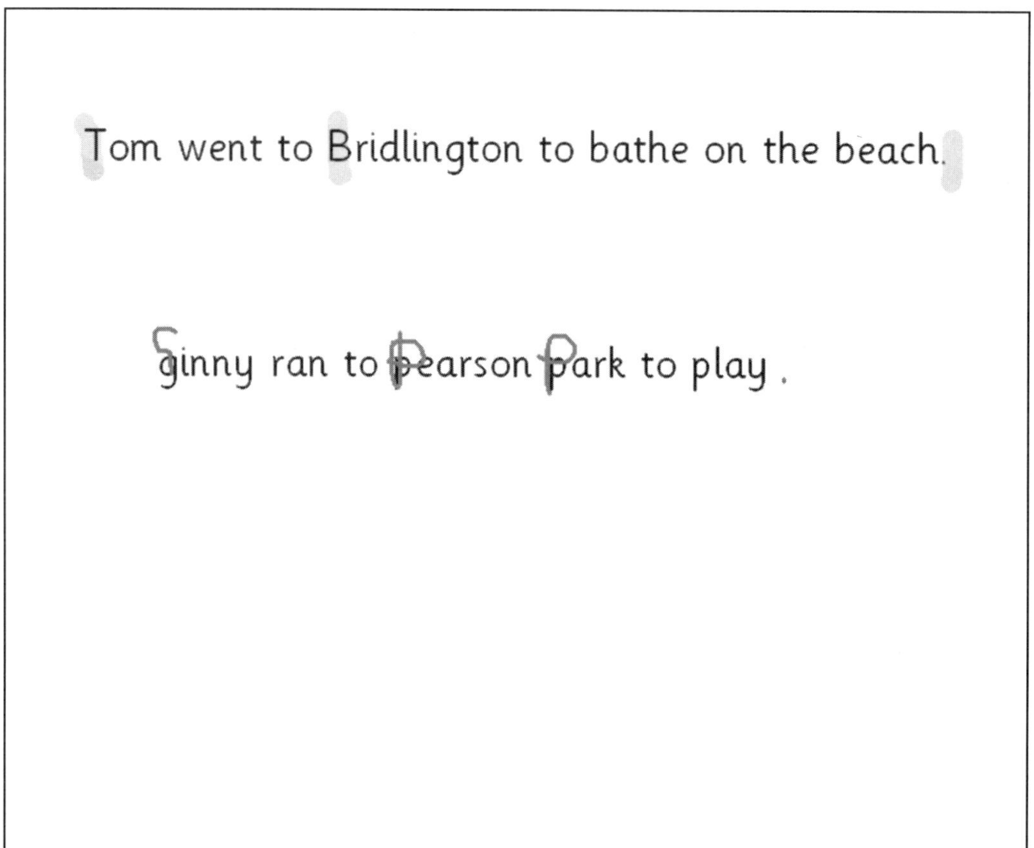

Figure 7

6 Highlight sentences in text using the highlighter tool. Stress the term 'sentence'.

7 Create a line of writing and display it on the IWB, then discuss that a line of text is not necessarily a sentence.

8 Create text on the IWB with missing full stops. Invite the children to insert them using the pen tool.

9 Start sentences with capital 'I'. Practise this by overwriting a sentence beginning with a lower-case 'i'. Use the pen tool for this.

Term 2 Sentence level work

Grammatical awareness

1 Read text written on the IWB screen. Check that it makes sense. Annotate as desired.

2 Use grammatical awareness to predict what happens next in a text. Display text on the IWB and invite the children to say what happens next. You can model the answer for them or they can respond orally.

3 Read text displayed on the IWB and predict words from the grammar. Suggest alternatives and write them on the board.

Sentence construction and punctuation

4 Recognise full stops and capital letters by adding them into text on a flipchart/notebook or highlighting them in text.

5 Highlight sentences on a flipchart and add a full stop when necessary. (The text should be created without full stops.)

6 Identify sentences in text by highlighting them. Notice capitals and full stops.

7 Punctuate a passage, replacing lower-case 'i' with a capital 'I'. Use the rub out tool if you have written freehand, or annotate over text. (Note that the text will have been created using lower-case 'i'.)

Term 3 Sentence level work

Grammatical awareness

1 Read text written on the IWB screen. Check that it makes sense. Annotate as desired.

2 Use grammatical awareness to predict what happens next in a text. Display text on the IWB and invite the children to say what happens next. You can model the answer for them or they can respond orally.

3 Read text aloud, with appropriate expression – pausing at full stops and raising your voice for questions. Use the IWB to display the text and annotate appropriately.

4 Reorder sentences using the select tool. Unscramble a set of words to create a sentence. You could also try the shareware software called *Hot Potatoes*

(which can be found on **www.halfbakedsoftware.com**), which allows you to create drag and drop exercises in the same manner.

Sentence construction and punctuation

5 Practise using capital letters for other rules of capitalisation. Do this by reading passages with the capital letters missing and then annotate them.

7 Add question marks to question sentences. Create a text of statements and questions and ask the children to annotate or mark the sentences which ask a question.

Term 1 Text level work

Reading comprehension

1 Display a variety of text on screen and annotate it or control it (e.g. talking book). This relates to shared and guided reading.

3 Check the meanings of unfamiliar words from displayed text. You could highlight unfamiliar words to elicit prediction of meanings. Text could be inserted or viewed from the Internet.

4 On the IWB, display text with which the children are familiar and discuss how the oral version differs from the written one. Use the pen or highlighter tool appropriately.

5 Describe settings as taken from text. Write about or draw your own settings on a flipchart. Annotate appropriately. If possible, relate the description of settings to peers. There is scope here for teacher and pupil modelling.

6 Recite a text on screen and add extra words, phrases or rhymes. You could use a sequence of flipcharts/notebook pages to do this by having an original piece of text on one page and then making alterations or additions to the text on subsequent pages.

Writing composition

8 On a flipchart, carry out spelling pattern activities, e.g. use the undo tool to sequence how a word is spelt. (Write out a word, look at it, undo each letter and ask the children to spell the word letter by letter. Use the redo tool to show each letter.) You could also highlight sections of the word in order to break it down into parts that will help build up the pattern of spelling for that particular word.

9 Ask the children, as a group, to come up to the IWB and write or talk about personal experiences related to incidents taken from a text. You could act as scribe, if necessary.

10 Display a rhyme or patterned text and annotate it appropriately so that children can use the ideas in their own writing.

11 On a flipchart, make a simple storybook modelled on a basic text convention (e.g. display captions, titles and layouts) and create a flipchart/notebook page to act as a template. The children can move the captions and titles, etc. into the correct position on the template using the select tool.

Reading comprehension

12 Create labels and captions. (You model them on the IWB and the children create them on a computer.) A group could work at the IWB to create a label, say for a picture of their classroom. They could use the select tool to match words to the correct picture or parts of a picture.

13 Read instructions and, in groups, make simple lists. These can be displayed on the IWB and actually be created by a group of children working at the board.

Writing composition

14 The children can come out to the board and add captions to pictures. They could do this with help if actual writing is a challenge. The teacher could also write what a child says using the character recognition tool.

15 Lists could be written on the IWB and arranged in order of importance using the select tool. The teacher or child could model this.

16 Groups of children could come out to the board and write or draw instructions for each other to carry out.

Term 2 Text level work

Reading comprehension

1 Use the IWB to display text and annotate it appropriately. You could use a talking book for this.

2 From the displayed text, you can identify unfamiliar words and invite the children to predict meanings by applying phonological, grammatical and graphic knowledge (use the pen or highlighter tool).

3 The class could read a book on screen with the aim of focussing attention and eliciting preferences. (Use of the Internet to show a chosen text would be appropriate.)

4 Retell a story, putting it in the correct order. Create text that summarises a story and, using the select tool, arrange it in the correct order. Each section of text will have to be created separately.

5 Identify the key features of a story by highlighting aspects of it displayed as text on the IWB. The children could come out and do an oral retelling.

6 Create flipcharts/notebook pages on different story themes and display them. Read them out and compare them. Keep them as a record of stories you have read.

7 Highlight causes and incidents in a story using the highlighter tool.

8 Use a flipchart to discuss character, both appearance and personality. Do this by displaying pictures of characters or by using the highlighter tool to show words that reveal aspects of character (see Figure 8).

Figure 8

9 Consider what these characters might say. Link speech bubbles to the characters. Create drawings/images of these characters and then add blank speech bubbles and get the children to say or write what is being said. You could copy the callouts from Word to do this. The Promethean Resource Library has a few of these in its default image library.

10 Identify and compare beginnings and endings in different stories. You could do this by creating beginnings and endings of stories, displaying them on the board and then annotating them appropriately. A collection of these beginnings and endings can be made and used as a reference.

11 Read poems from the IWB. Create actions from the words. Simply displaying text on a large screen is a vast improvement on previous methods of display, especially when it can be written over and saved. The Internet is a useful source of such material.

Writing composition

12 Use a flipchart/notebook to aid spelling, e.g. split up a word into syllables and then join them together using the select tool. Create each syllable separately to do this.

13 Add to text on a flipchart, e.g. add more lines or verses to a poem, identify alliteration or add new rhyming words. You could use the select tool to drag up pre-written text into a passage of text.

14 Outline a story plot by selecting and ordering pictures and captions. Using a Promethean board, you could add to an annotation library and then select stored pictures (drawings, not images) from it. You could draw arrows to indicate a sequence and link them to words or pictures. You would use the gallery to do this on a SMART board.

15 As a group, write about a character on an IWB, concentrating on appearance and personality. Use a stored picture to act as a stimulus. This could also be a whole-class activity with you, the teacher, modelling the writing.

16 Use the elements of story writing as laid down in a flow diagram, e.g. to create a story plan as a group on an IWB.

Reading comprehension

17 Learn about fiction and non-fiction by looking at various texts of the two types and displaying them on the IWB and comparing and contrasting them.

18 Read on screen a non-fiction book or information CD-ROM. Find out information from the contents you have displayed. Annotate appropriately.

19 Scan the covers and blurb of a book and display them on the IWB. Invite the children to predict what the book is about from what they see.

20 Create a page in the style of a dictionary and display it on screen to show the class the alphabetical organisation of a dictionary. Using the *Cambridge Learner's Dictionary* CD-ROM by installing it on your display computer is a useful asset. It is cheap and is distributed by Granada Learning.

21 Create a flipchart/notebook on how to use contents pages, indexes, etc. Annotate where necessary. You could use a document camera here to show such pages, but they would be in video mode.

Writing composition

22 Write labels or captions for images or drawings created on a flipchart/notebook. You could paste an image onto the IWB screen and then create movable labels to match parts of the picture or pictures.

23 Write an extended caption related to a picture or photograph created on a flipchart/notebook. Children could come out to the board in groups and do this as a collaborative piece of work.

24 Write a simple non-chronological report on the board, e.g. create a shopping list from a picture prompt of a supermarket as shown on a flipchart. This could be a group activity done at the board.

Term 3 Text level work

Reading comprehension

Much of this section has been visited by references to previous terms. Additional ideas stem from the following numbers.

4 Reading text from a flipchart/notebook and using the curtain or spotlight tool would serve to focus the children on reading the text.

5 & 6 In retelling stories, children could be encouraged to write the main parts of a story on an IWB after talking it through in groups. You could also act as scribe.

7 Store a collection of pages and 'blurbs' on a flipchart and use them to predict the content of unfamiliar stories. You might scan these into your computer, but be aware of copyright issues.

8 Display text extracts on the IWB that deal with different story settings and compare them. Annotate appropriately.

9 Read out loud a variety of poems as displayed on the IWB.

10 Create a template of a choice chart on the IWB and fill in children's preferences and themes related to stories and poems.

11 Create a flipchart collection of favourite poems and read and annotate accordingly. Write about significant incidents from stories. You could use a writing frame that can be paper or electronically based to do this. If stored electronically, then it can be displayed and annotated over.

Writing composition

12 Use a flipchart to aid spelling, e.g. split up a word into syllables and then join them together using the select tool. Create your syllables separately so you can move them about.

13 Model writing on the IWB related to significant incidents in stories. Children could display work written in Word and show it to the rest of the class, annotating as they go along.

14 The children could work in groups to describe a setting, and demonstrate their results on the IWB. They could use other computers and then load the text onto the computer running the IWB. One group can work at the board.

15 Use a poem written on a flipchart/notebook and add to it or alter it using the rub out (handwritten) or edit (printed text) tool. Alternatively, you could simply add to it on another page.

16 Model the creation of a poem using the IWB, then create a poem using pre-written but jumbled up phrases or sentences and moving them with the select tool. All phrases must be created separately.

Reading comprehension

17 Compare non-fiction texts on a similar theme, using the IWB to show the text and illustrate how the information can look different.

18 Read an account from text on the IWB and highlight words that show a generic structure, e.g. sequences of events as indicated by highlighted words like 'first', 'next', 'when', 'after'.

19 Use displayed text and ask questions about it. Use the highlighter tool to show the relevant parts of text.

Writing composition

20 Collectively, write a simple story or sequence of events, e.g. 'Our day at school'. The children will be at the board, annotating or writing their ideas on it.

21 Create texts that give information, including labelled diagrams, on the IWB. Elicit from the children the style and language of such texts to help them write a class book, e.g. 'What we know about our pets'.

22 You can model the creation of a set of questions prior to reading for information. Show an image about a given subject and act as scribe on the IWB to record answers.

Term 1 Word level work

Phonological awareness, phonics and spelling

1 Revise work as for Year 1, as laid down in the NLS handbook. The references to IWBs are in the Year 1, Term 3, Word level work.

2 Display a list of long vowel phoneme words on the IWB and ask the children to highlight the vowels. Turn to a new flipchart/notebook page showing the same words but with the vowels missing. Get the children to insert them using the pen tool.

3 Display a text on the IWB and then ask the children to highlight phonemes of required words. Ask them to join phonemes together using the select tool. Appendix List 3, p.64 of the NLS handbook is the source of the phonemes.

4 Classify words with different spellings but the same sound, e.g. 'steak' and 'stake'. Match them up using the select tool. You could also write out the meanings and mix and match them using the select tool.

Word recognition, graphic knowledge and spelling

5 You can create flipcharts/notebook files with the words from NLS handbook Appendix List 1 and read them, arrange them in alphabetical order, split them in half and join the halves, or put them into sentences. All of these can be done in a flipchart/notebook using the select tool.

6 Read on sight high-frequency words as identified on the IWB (via graded texts).

7 Practise plurals ('s'), past tense ('ed') and present tense ('ing') by adding these suffixes to the ends of words. You would do this on the IWB by using the select tool to match them up with the beginnings of words.

8 Create a flipchart/notebook page with the words 'vowel' and 'consonant' written on it. Read it for sight vocabulary. Use the undo tool to rub out all but the first letter. Ask the children to spell the word letter by letter, revealing the correct letter as you go along, using the redo tool. This works well on Promethean and SMART boards. It is easier to do this freehand than in print.

9 Make a list of the common irregular words from Appendix 1 of the NLS handbook and then apply the techniques mentioned in number 5. An extra technique would be to use the select tool to add the words to an appropriate image.

Vocabulary extension

10 Create a flipchart/notebook to store any new words you come across and refer to it in your literacy lesson from time to time, using the flipchart techniques mentioned in number 5. You can also match them to any images you find on the Internet.

Handwriting

11 & 12 You can practise and demonstrate handwriting on the IWB if you can make lined backgrounds. On a Promethean board, you have tiles that are insertable pages, and some of these are handwriting guide lines. A SMART board has a similar feature via its gallery icon. You simply load them up and start to model your handwriting. The main tasks here are to practise the four basic joins. You could model handwriting patterns on the board for the children to see and copy (see figure 9).

Figure 9

Term 2 Word level work

Phonological awareness, phonics and spelling

1 This relates to the revision of long vowel phonemes from Year 1 and has been covered in that year.

2 & 3 For these, you can create flipcharts/notebook files with words containing the phonemes 'air' or 'er' (NLS handbook Appendix List 3) or digraphs 'wh', 'ph', 'ch' and then ask the children to highlight them. You can split the words up and use the select tool to join them together. You can put the words into sentences or the children can do it on the IWB instead of you doing the modelling.

4 To create compound words, use the flipchart select tool to join halves of words together. Put the words into sentences by using cloze procedure and dragging the correct word into a missing space. Compound words could also be matched to appropriate images using the select tool.

5 Practise syllables by highlighter them on a flipchart. Create a piece of text on the IWB with the words you have practised on and then ask the children to annotate and highlight the required syllables.

Word recognition, graphic knowledge and spelling

Ideas for numbers 6, 7 and 9 have been covered in the first term's word recognition section and relate to reading sight words displayed on the IWB from NLS handbook Appendix List 1.

8 Use the select tool to add the negative prefixes 'un' and 'dis' to words. Reshape sentences by changing them from the positive to the negative by writing 'un' or 'dis' before the chosen word. You would use the pen tool for this.

Vocabulary extension

10 Create topic collections of words related to Year 2 work linked to sound files. You do this by creating links to sound files so that when you select a word it speaks to you. This is done easily on a Promethean whiteboard or using Granada Writer/Textease. Both methods are equally effective. SMART has recently brought out amended software that has this ability to hyperlink, but it uses links on a separate page rather than cutting from the word itself.

11 Use a flipchart/notebook and the select tool to match up words and their opposites (antonyms).

Handwriting

Use the IWB to practise the four basic handwriting joins. (More detailed references are dealt with in the NLS handbook.) Remember to use pages with lines on to guide your modelling of these patterns.

Term 3 Word level work

Phonological awareness, phonics and spelling

This is mainly concerned with revision of the previous five terms, and ideas for numbers 1 and 2 have therefore already been covered.

3 Use the highlight tool to mark the phonemes 'ear' and 'ea'. Create pages on the IWB with words containing these phonemes and highlight them using the highlighter tool. Alternately, display sentences or text and ask the children to annotate over the required phonemes.

Word recognition, graphic knowledge and spelling

There is repetition of work for numbers 4 and 5 relating to reading and spelling high-frequency words from NLS handbook Appendix List 1.

6 Look at words with the same spelling patterns but different sounds. Collect families of these words. Mix them up on a flipchart/notebook file and then use the select tool to match them up. The meanings of the words could also be matched up with the words themselves.

7 Create a word list and add the suffixes 'ful' and 'ly' to them using the select tool. Use the pen or highlighter tool to mark these suffixes on a given IWB text.

8 Display the common irregular words from Appendix List 1 and read them, then ask the children to come out to the IWB and spell them. They could also say them and you can write them out.

Vocabulary extension

9 Collect new words on an IWB flipchart and save them to refer to periodically.

10 Use synonyms. You could create a text on a flipchart and then use the highlighter tool to mark the appropriate synonyms. These could be saved on IWB pages and revisited periodically.

Handwriting

12 You could use a tiled background or lined paper to practise the phonic and spelling patterns required in this section. Again, this is the practice of the four basic handwriting joins.

Term 1 Sentence level work

Grammatical awareness

1 Create a flipchart/notebook file with text on it and get the children to decipher new and unfamiliar words using awareness of grammar. Children could annotate or highlight new words.

2 Create a flipchart/notebook file that has examples of words and phrases that link sentences, e.g. after, meanwhile, before, then, next, after a while. Children could read the text with you and then highlight the conjunctions. On another page, write sentences and use the select tool to link them with a joining word from a list of conjunctions you have created.

Sentence construction and punctuation

3 Identify commas and exclamation marks. Create a flipchart/notebook file with text on it and then get the children to annotate over it, highlighting the commas and exclamation marks. They could then be challenged to add commas and exclamation marks to text that has them omitted.

5 Work on capital letters by correcting flipchart passages with capital letters missing. You would use the pen tool for this.

6 You can model using organisational devices by creating a flipchart with arrows, lines, boxes, etc., to show sequencing and relationships. Alternatively, there is a super program called *Kidspiration* that will do the job for you. There's also an application called SMART Ideas from the makers of SMART boards which will do similar things and which can be downloaded from the SMART website for a 30-day trial period.

Term 2 Sentence level work

Grammatical awareness

1 & 2 As in the previous section, by displaying text on the large IWB screen, children can practise predicting and saying unfamiliar words and beginning to read with intonation and expression.

3 Check a written text for accuracy, understanding and agreement. Display a text with errors in it and challenge the children to spot them using the annotate (pen) or highlighter tool.

4 Be aware of how to match verbs to nouns/pronouns, making sure of agreement. You could do this by asking which pronoun or noun matches the correct verb, e.g. 'I' matches 'am', 'the children' matches 'are'. Text displayed on the IWB could be annotated appropriately or arrows drawn to show which noun or pronoun is linked with which verb.

5 Use the present and past tense of verbs correctly. Change text into past or present by writing over printed text on a flipchart page. You could create a cloze procedure exercise to either drag in correctly tensed words or write in the answers.

Sentence construction and punctuation

6 Identify or insert speech marks. This could be done simply by annotating over a Word document with missing speech marks that you have created for this purpose and displayed on the IWB. You could draw speech bubbles on screen and get the children to fill them in. You could also link the text to sound files (use Promethean software or Granada Writer/Textease).

7 Use the flipchart toolbar to highlight a range of ways of presenting texts. You could add arrows or speech bubbles to text (see Figure 10). You could go into mouse mode so that you actually control an application. You could then use the on-screen keyboard or text recognition to type in text, enlarge headings or change the colour of fonts. You would really be demonstrating the features of a word processor on an IWB by switching between mouse and annotate mode.

8 Use commas in a list. Write out some text and get the children to add commas where they find a list.

9 Write simple sentences correctly, including using capital letters and full stops. Simply ask the children, singly or in groups (helped by you or a teaching assistant, if available), to come out to the IWB and write out sentences that are correctly punctuated and make sense.

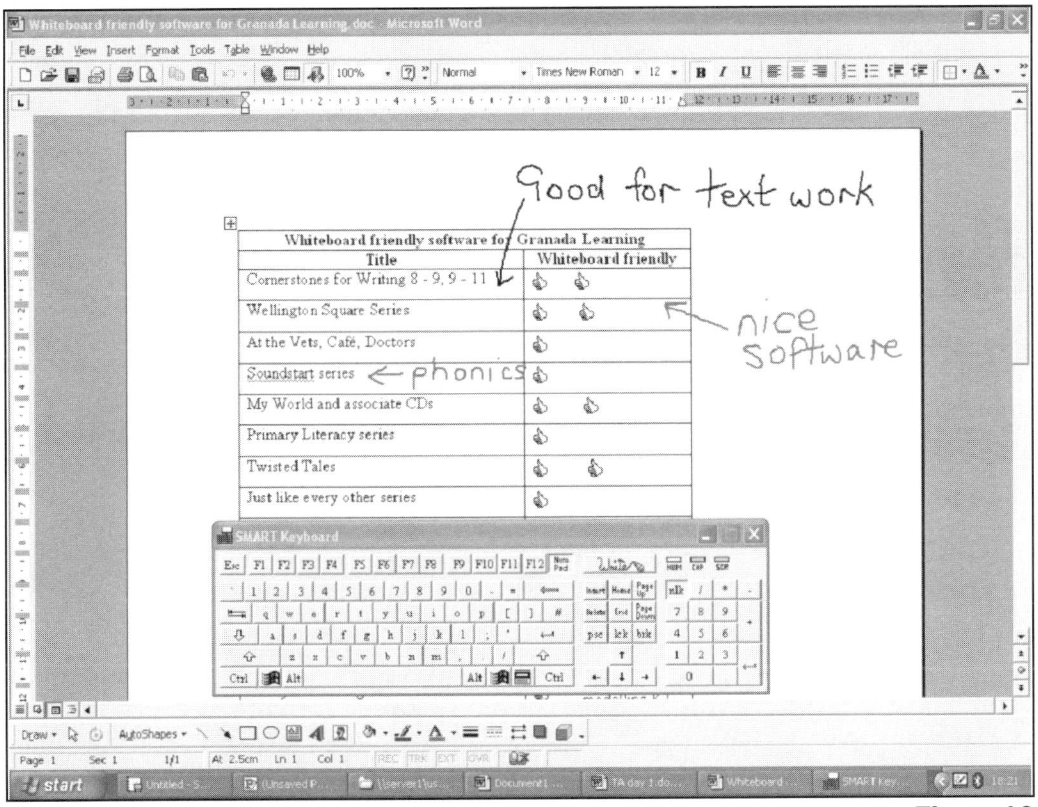

Figure 10

Term 3 Sentence level work

Grammatical awareness

1 Place text on the IWB screen and everybody reads from it, with emphasis on intonation and awareness of grammar. Annotate or highlight as desired.

2 Create a flipchart/notebook file with a mix of pronouns and nouns and match them to listed verbs, e.g. I am, we are, the cat is, etc. Use the select tool to match, say, 'I' to 'am'. On a separate page, get the children to do the same, but ask them to see if they can add anything else to make a proper sentence. Use the pen tool for this.

3 Use past and present tenses correctly. Match the correct forms by using the select tool, e.g. 'catch' links with 'caught'. You could also create a table to sort a mixture of present and past tense verbs using the select tool.

Sentence construction and punctuation

4 Create some text with listed words on an IWB and ask the children to add commas where they have been omitted.

5 Invite the children to come out to the IWB and write sentences in groups, putting in capital letters and full stops. (You can train the children to write a little larger on screen by using a flipchart with lines on it.)

6 Turn a statement into a question using 'what', 'where', 'when' and adding question marks. You can model this by annotating over some text or by

writing a new 'asking' sentence. You could also use the select tool to drag statements and their corresponding question sentences together.

7 Read texts on the IWB and compare a variety of forms of question. The children could highlight various forms of question outlined in a text, e.g. asking for help, asking the time, asking someone to be quiet.

Term 1 Text level work

Fiction and Poetry

Reading comprehension

1 Use the IWB simply to display text so everyone can see it – a huge advantage over a big book. Annotate and control appropriately.

2 Use displayed text on the IWB to highlight unfamiliar words, and get the children to predict their meanings.

3 Use the IWB to display text so that everyone can see it, and then compare the text with an oral recount, making use of formal story elements in retelling.

4 Understand sequential relationships, i.e. what happened next. Read text on screen to elicit either oral or written answers from the children on the IWB. You could also display a variety of answers for the children to highlight or select.

5 Discuss reasons for events in stories after having read them on screen. Highlight relevant keywords and use them as a stimulus for writing.

6 Discuss story themes and link to own experiences, e.g. illness, getting lost. You'll need text and images on a flipchart to stimulate discussion.

7 Read favourite poems and learn them by heart. Display copies on an IWB (e.g. from the Internet) and annotate appropriately. Remember to use commercial materials to comply with copyright.

Writing composition

9 Use text on the IWB to apply phonological and graphic knowledge and sight vocabulary to spell words properly. Words can be highlighted or annotated over.

10 Look at the structure of a displayed story and annotate important points (it will have to be abridged so it displays well on the IWB). From that, the children can write about their own experiences in the same form. They could do this in groups at a computer using an electronic template.

11 Use language of time to sequence events. Identify these from displayed text on the IWB, or give time phrases to be included in a sentence, and the children come to the board to finish them off, e.g. 'when I had finished', 'suddenly'. (Alternative sentence endings could be added using the select tool.)

12 Create new poems from old ones. Use a flipchart to display an original poem, then children can add their own work. The children could put in missing words or create new verses.

Non-fiction

Reading comprehension

13. Read instructions displayed on the IWB and then carry out the activity. You could also ask the children to annotate over the instructions to break down how such text is constructed.

14. Create a list on a flipchart and then highlight its structural features.

Writing composition

15. Create instructions on the IWB as a group, e.g. how to make a cup of tea.

16. Organise instructions sequentially. Model text on a flipchart/notebook screen with instructions mixed up, and get the children to put the instructions in the right order using the select tool

17. Create a drawing and ask the children to label it as if it were an instructional diagram. Use the arrow and box tool on the IWB to do this. You can also simply use the pen tool.

Term 2 text level work

Fiction and Poetry

Reading comprehension

Numbers 1 and 2 have been covered in Term 1.

3 Discuss and compare story themes by writing out assorted extracts on the IWB and getting the children to identify the themes. You could do one per flipchart/notebook page, with images inserted to help. The children could come out to the board and write what the theme is.

4 Create brief story extracts and get the children to finish them (predict the ending) orally or in groups at the board.

5 Make images on a flipchart showing different story settings with some description. Get the children to highlight the keywords and then add to the description orally or at the IWB.

6 Identify characters from images or text on a flipchart and get the children to either highlight keywords or create arrows and boxes to identify characteristics (physical and related to perceived personality).

8 Write out a child's poem on the IWB and invite the child (or children) to come out and read it to the class. In case of stage fright, get two or more children to help. Children could create their own word-processed poem and save it to disk to be shown to the class later on the IWB. This might be an ideal homework activity

9 Examine a poem and annotate it or highlight aspects of it to study rhyming patterns.

11 Read scanned or typed-in poems and use common keywords such as 'poet', 'verse', 'rhyme' and say to where in a poem they refer.

Writing composition

13 Choose a story setting displayed on an IWB to stimulate the creation of a story that is different from the original. The IWB is there to add initial impetus and, after suitable annotation by the teacher and children, the children can attempt their own story settings.

14 Write on the IWB about a character you have seen or discussed. This would be a group activity, with children discussing keywords and writing them on the board to build up a draft picture of the character in question. They can then either write up the description on the board with help, or work at a computer, save their work to disk, load it onto the display computer and then show it to the rest of the class.

15 Show a poem on the IWB and get the children to write a different ending for it. (This can be done as a group.) Lines can be altered, captions added and all of it can be saved for later use.

Non-fiction

Reading comprehension

16 Use a dictionary on screen (e.g. DK *My First Amazing Dictionary* or the *Cambridge Learner's Dictionary*). Navigate a CD-ROM to find information (e.g. *Oxford Children's Encyclopaedia* on CD-ROM). Annotate appropriately. Alternatively, create your own dictionary page and highlight the relevant features.

17 Display some simple word definitions on the IWB and then explore them by annotating or highlighting relevant text. You could jumble them up and then use the select tool to match them back together.

18 Identify what an index or directory is by creating one on a flipchart and asking relevant questions (see Figure 11). Annotate and highlight as appropriate.

19 Create and read flow charts using an IWB. You can save the pages you have created as blanks and fill them in with your own content. You can then get the children to follow them and make explanations. Kidspiration by Tag Learning or SMART Ideas is a useful application for this purpose.

Writing composition

20 In a group at the IWB, ask the children to design a dictionary entry. You could have a couple of jumbled up ones prepared to model with and then use the select tool to put them together correctly.

21 Give the children a task involving a sequence, e.g. how to repair a puncture, and then ask them to create a flow chart on the IWB to explain it.

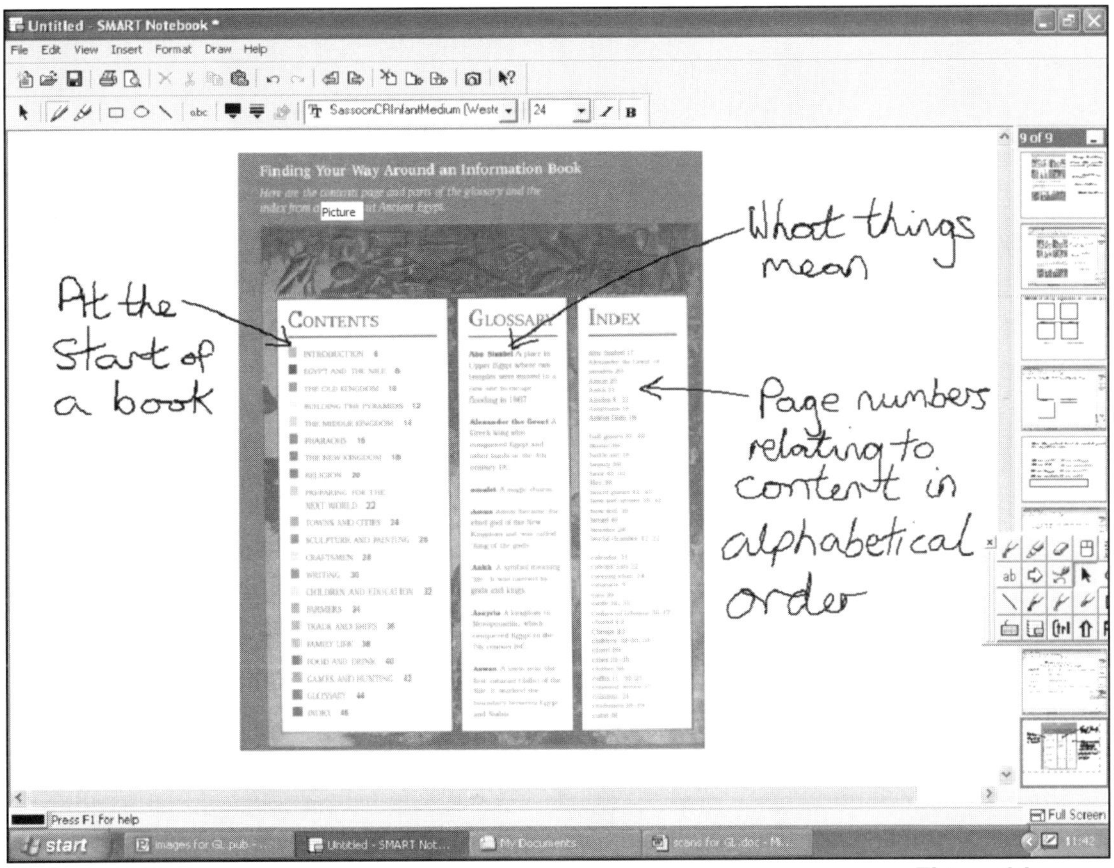

Figure 11

Term 3 Text level work

Fiction and Poetry

Reading comprehension

Numbers 1 to 3 have been covered previously in Terms 1 and 2.

4 Prepare text extracts from different books by the same author on a flipchart and discuss settings, characters and themes. Annotate and highlight.

5 Read about authors from an inserted (scanned) book cover to become aware of authorship and publication. Annotate and highlight.

6 Extracts of humourous text and poems are displayed on a flipchart/notebook file. Elicit a response from the children either orally or by annotation, e.g. 'What words make the text funny?'

8 Display poems about humour and poetical sound effects. Read them out loud and analyse by annotating and highlighting. These can also be extended or completed in a cloze style of exercise using either the pen or select tool. The pen tool writes in the missing space and the select tool moves pre-created text into a given space.

Writing composition

11 Use a humorous verse created on a flipchart/notebook file and model changing it around on a blank chart. Get the children to write their own and ask one or more groups to write it on the IWB. The Internet is a possible source for this.

12 Create a book evaluation as a group on a flipchart/notebook file.

Non-fiction

Reading comprehension

13 Write the words 'fact', 'fiction' and 'non-fiction' on the board and then write their meanings in a mixed-up order. Ask the children to match them up using the select tool.

14 Tell the children the title of a non-fiction text and then ask them to create questions about it. You can then read the text with the children on screen.

15 Display a contents page and index and highlight elements of them to explain what they do.

16 Display text or sentences on a flipchart and get the children to highlight keywords.

17 Create a sequence of flipchart/notebook pages with a title, contents page, illustrations and chapter headings and ask the children to speculate what the book may be about.

18 Evaluate a text on a flipchart to see how useful it is, e.g. for instructions, are they clear and concise? You could use a voting system (Promethean has 'Activ Vote', for example).

19 Make a table about a non-fiction text on a flipchart/notebook file with suitable headings. Ask the children to remember key points under the headings you have chosen. You can model the writing.

20 Ask the children to write a non-fiction text after having used the IWB to show the use of headings, sub-headings and captions.

21 Re-sort a jumbled, short, non-chronological report. Rearrange the report appropriately and annotate where necessary, using the select tool.

Term 1 Word level work

Phonics, spelling and vocabulary

Numbers 1, 2 and 3 are revision areas and have already been covered. This consists of the revision of phonemic work and knowledge of the high-frequency words in Appendix List 1 of the NLS handbook. You could join halves of words or highlight beginnings and endings. See Appendix List 3 for the phonemic work (p.64 of NLS handbook).

4 Discriminate syllables. Split words up into syllables using the highlighter tool or join them up using the select tool. (Remember to create the syllables separately so they can be moved.)

Spelling strategies

5 Identify misspelt words by creating text in a flipchart with misspelt words. The children have to identify them using the annotation tool.

6 Use independent spelling strategies:

- read out aloud from a flipchart/notebook file list
- highlight letter strings (highlight tool)
- create words with similar patterns and meanings (medicine, medical); add beginnings and endings to words using the select tool
- spell by analogy (light, fright); use the same technique as mentioned previously (add 'ight' to various letters using either the pen or select tool).
- Display word banks and dictionaries and annotate as desired.

7 Use the undo or redo tool to practise look, cover, say and check strategies. You could use the curtain tool to cover a spelling, or the rubber tool to erase a word after having seen it, and then get the children to rewrite it.

Spelling conventions and rules

8 Adding 'ing' to verbs. You can write a series of verbs on a chart and add 'ing' using the select tool. You model and explain any relevant changes using the pen tool to alter any words.

9 Investigate the 'le' spelling pattern. Create a text with 'le' spellings and highlight and annotate. You could split words up with missing 'le' endings and then use the select tool to join them up. This kind of activity can also be created using a word processor application like Granada Writer or Textease (Studio).

10 Add common prefixes 'un', 'de', 'dis', 're', 'pre' to the beginnings of words using the select tool on the IWB, e.g. 'un' can be added to 'happy' to make 'unhappy'.

11 Use prefixes to create opposites, e.g. appear/disappear. Create a selection of words on the IWB and add prefixes using the select tool. Alternatively, you could match opposites using the select tool.

Vocabulary extension

13 Make, maintain and save a new word flipchart/notebook file and visit it regularly to sight-read and carry out the look, cover, say, write technique. On a flipchart/notebook file it would be look, rub out, say then come out and use the pen tool to spell.

14 Read a sentence and infer the meaning of a word from it by writing it on a flipchart/notebook file and highlighting any key words or phrases to help find the meaning (in context).

15 Create a flipchart to illustrate the work of a dictionary. You'll need to make a dictionary-type page to illustrate how it works. Use annotations or highlighter to model explanations. Visiting **www.gridclub.com** and clicking on the 'Look it up' tab could help as it leads you to a collection of dictionary work.

17 Generate synonyms for high-frequency words, e.g. big, little, like, nasty. This would be a good brainstorming session for groups at the IWB. You could use the rectangle boxes and arrows to create flow diagram pages to put your words in.

18 Use the method mentioned in number 13 to learn how to spell the word 'synonym'.

19 Write out the vocabulary words 'said', 'replied', 'asked' and 'told' on the IWB, mixed with other words, and ask the children to group them according to 'speech words'. This can be done for other word groups. Use the select tool for this activity.

Handwriting

This relates to more work on basic joins using a tiled background of guide lines (p.33 of the NLS handbook).

Term 2 Word level work

Numbers 1 to 7 have already been covered (see word work from Year 2 and Year 3, Term 1) and include 'Revision and consolidation from KS1' and 'Spelling strategies'.

Spelling conventions and rules

8 Use a flipchart to show how words change when 'er', 'est' and 'y' are added, e.g. use the select tool to add 'er' to 'warm', 'big', etc. Include extra letters on the flipchart, as these will need to be added in some cases (e.g. 'g' to 'bigger'). Alternatively, you could use the pen tool to insert additional letters.

9 Investigate nouns plus 's' and rules. Create a flipchart/notebook file containing a list of nouns and use the select tool to attach an 's'. What happens to words ending in 'y'? Use the pen tool to adjust any words. You'll need to model the explanation on the IWB.

10 Work on silent letters, e.g. 'knee', 'wrinkle', 'gnat'. Create a flipchart that has 'kn' written on it and then use the select tool to add it to various graphemes, e.g. 'ee', 'at', 'ot', etc. Model putting them in a sentence, then get the children to do it away from the IWB (see Figure 12).

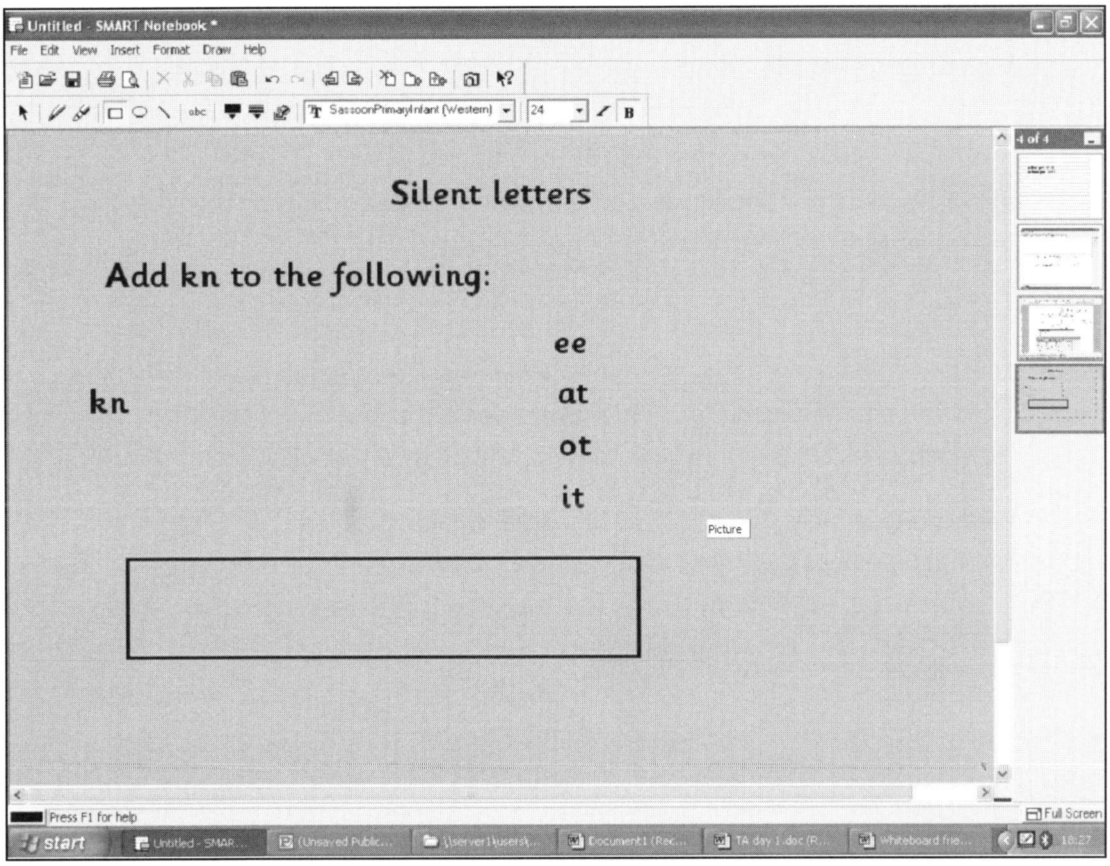

Figure 12

11 View the words 'singular' and 'plural' on an IWB and use the undo tool to spell them out.

12 Join the halves of compound words together on a flipchart. Each item of text needs to be created separately so it can be moved about on its own. Consider using Granada Writer or Textease (Studio) for this.

13 Join the suffixes 'ly', 'ful' and 'less' to words on an IWB by using the select tool to match them up.

14 Generate new words using suffixes, e.g. add 'ly' to 'proud' to get 'proudly'. Create a list of such words on the IWB and then use the select tool to join them together to make the new word.

15 Match a contracted word to one that isn't contracted, using the select tool. Model writing contractions on a flipchart. Identify contractions in text by using the highlighter tool. You can also use the pen tool to overwrite words that need to be made into contractions.

16 Discuss the word 'suffix' and write a definition of it on the board. Write some words that have suffixes and get the children to highlight the suffixed parts of words.

Vocabulary extension

19 Use a dictionary CD-ROM, e.g. DK's *Children's Dictionary*, or the Internet to explore dictionary definitions. Show this on the IWB and annotate accordingly. Granada Learning has a dictionary called the *Cambridge Learner's Dictionary* which is very useful.

20 Model creating your own definitions for a given word on a flipchart/notebook file.

23 Explore alphabetical organisation using the first two letters of words. Write out words on the flipchart and select them in the right order accordingly, e.g. words beginning with 'sa', 'sc', 'su', 'si', etc.

24 Explore opposites by matching them up on a flipchart, using the select tool.

Handwriting

It's very useful to practise handwriting on an IWB because words that are well formed have a greater chance of being displayed correctly via character recognition.

Work on basic handwriting joins (p.35 of the NLS handbook) using a tiled background (one with guide lines).

Term 3 Word level work

Numbers 1 to 7 have already been covered (see word work from Year 2 and Year 3, Term 1) and include 'Revision and consolidation from KS1' and 'Spelling strategies'.

Spelling conventions and rules

8 Spot short words within longer ones. Use the highlighter or pen tool for this exercise.

9 Use the prefixes 'mis', 'non', 'ex', 'co' and 'anti' to generate new words. You can match these prefixes up with parts of other words using the select tool. You could also write out a piece of text and get children to highlight any prefixes they spot.

10 Linked to number 9, children can create new words from word roots using their knowledge of these prefixes, e.g. 'lead' changes to 'mislead' and 'sense' changes to 'nonsense'. Use the select tool for this activity. You also need to explain the meaning of 'ex' or 'mis' so the children can get clues to the meaning of words. You could write words like 'extend' or 'explode' on the IWB, and brainstorm meanings with the children. Use different coloured pens to show additions and changes.

11 Investigate more contractions, e.g. couldn't. You could do as above by matching the contracted word to the elongated version. Use the select tool to do this.

Vocabulary extension

12 Continue to collect new words to be stored on a flipchart for further revisits.

13 Create a synonym list for the 'spoken' word, e.g. shouted, cried, yelled, squealed. Create a word list of these on a flipchart/notebook file and then write out some sentences. Invite the children to come out and rub out/delete a word and substitute it from the word list. A pen tool could also be used to overwrite it.

14 Explore homonyms that have the same spelling but not the same meaning. Match the various meanings to the words, using the select tool, e.g. 'form' can link to the meanings 'shape' or 'document'.

16 Create a flipchart/notebook file of common expressions and display it. Annotate it as necessary.

Handwriting

Practise handwriting as defined on p.37 of the NLS handbook. Create a tiled background and practise the four basic joins.

Term 1 Sentence level work

Grammatical awareness

1 On the IWB, display text that contains new vocabulary, and ask the children to highlight it using the highlighter tool. Brainstorm and annotate the text with regard to its meaning, using strategies such as reading the context.

2 Read out loud texts on the IWB and take into account punctuation and grammar.

Fill in missing parts of grammar and punctuation (speech marks, exclamation marks, commas, etc.) from prepared flipcharts/notebook files, using the pen tool.

3 Look at verbs on the IWB, recognise them via the use of the highlighter tool and alter them in sentences to change meaning (by changing the tense, for example). Annotate over a verb or rub it out and write over it if you use the annotate mode (pen tool) on the IWB. If you have created text, you will have to write over it with the pen tool.

4 Use verbs more accurately by changing tenses. Use the select tool to match lists of verbs in different tenses, e.g. 'catch' with 'caught'. You could also display text on screen and then change it from the past to the present by annotating over the chosen verb. The reverse could also be done.

Sentence construction and punctuation

6 Practise the use of question marks and exclamation marks by adding them to sentences on an IWB.

7 Add speech marks to sentences on a flipchart or to a displayed document, using the pen tool.

8 Write the term 'speech mark' on the IWB and model an explanation.

9 Create a flipchart/notebook file to show a range of ways of presenting speech in text, e.g. speech bubbles, captions, headings. Create blanks of these for the children to fill in at the board. Show the children examples on screen and model some writing before the children come out to the board to do it themselves. The callouts from Word can be imported to add variety.

Term 2 Sentence level work

Grammatical awareness

2 Recognise adjectives in flipcharts by highlighter them in a sentence or displayed text on the IWB.

- Write a short list of nouns on the IWB and then match them up with appropriate qualifying adjectives using the select tool.
- Substitute adjectives by writing over them with an alternative. This can be done by annotating over Word. Alternatively, use the select tool to replace an adjective with an alternative from a list.
- Collect and classify adjectives by writing down a mixture of them on a flipchart/notebook file and then using the select tool to sort them out, e.g. by colour.

3 Explain the word 'adjective' by modelling its meaning on the IWB.

4 Create a flipchart to change sentences from singular to plural. You can do this by annotating over text or using the select tool to put in alternatives. You could also display a Word document with missing plurals and get the children to write them in using the pen tool.

Gather together examples of collective nouns and display them on the board. Write out some text with collective nouns in and highlight accordingly. You could also create a piece of cloze procedure text and add words using the select tool or write it in using the pen tool. 'ClozePro' by Cricksoft would be an ideal tool with which to do this.

5 Teach the children the meaning of 'singular' and 'plural' by modelling the meanings on the IWB. Invite children to come out and write with you on the board. You could link text to images for this, e.g. an image of a boy relates to the word 'boy'; an image of boys relates to the plural 'boys'.

Sentence construction and punctuation

6 Highlight commas in a text and discuss their uses. Add commas to displayed text that has the commas omitted, using the pen tool.

8 Create a piece of text that needs a variety of capital letters (not sentence starts) and then invite the children to come out to the IWB and annotate appropriately.

9 Write out sentences and get the children to cross out parts that are not essential to the meaning of the text.

10 Practise the declension of verbs from 1st and 2nd person to 3rd person. Create a flipchart/notebook file or a Word document and annotate over the verbs as they change from person to person, e.g. 'He goes', 'I go'. Children could write the numbers 1, 2 or 3 as necessary. Show texts that use the various persons, e.g. 'I' for letters or diaries; 'you' for instructions or directions; 'he', 'she', 'it', 'they' for narrative recounts.

11 Practise 'I am' and not 'we was', etc. Get the children to come out to the IWB and recognise errors in text by annotating or replacing words.

Term 3 Sentence level work

Grammatical awareness

2 Identify pronouns and understand their functions in sentences through:

- recognising them as replacements for nouns by substituting them for the nouns themselves on a flipchart. This can be done by simple annotation or highlighter.
- distinguishing between 'I', 'you', 'him' and possessive pronouns 'my', 'yours', 'hers' by putting them into a flipchart and then placing them in their correct family (possessive/not possessive) in a table. They could also simply be highlighted in written text.
- matching, for example, 'he' to a picture of a boy on a flipchart.
- discussing the gender issue of pronouns (p.36 of the NLS handbook) by using the method just described.

3 Using the select tool, drag the correct pronoun into a place that matches a verb, e.g. 'I' goes with 'am', 'we' goes with 'are', etc.

Sentence construction and punctuation

4 Type some text without speech marks into Word or place it on a flipchart and then invite the children to put in the speech marks and boundary marks using the pen tool.

5 In a flipchart, create text that needs conjunctions and get the children to add their own by annotation, e.g. 'if', 'so' ,'while', 'since', 'when'. This extends the use of conjunctions from the basic 'and' and 'then' words.

6 Make a flipchart collection of words that signal time, e.g. 'first', 'then', 'after', 'meanwhile', 'from', 'where'. Ask the children to work in a group at the IWB to create sentences containing these words. Encourage them to show their results to the rest of the class.

7 Practise reading texts with commas that mark grammatical boundaries. Display these via the whiteboard. Ask the children to insert commas into text using a pen tool.

Term 1 Text level work

Fiction and Poetry

Reading comprehension

1 Create story settings and elicit appropriate vocabulary. You'll need to collect descriptions of story settings that are either scanned (check on copyright), typed in Word, Granada Writer/Textease (Studio) or created on a flipchart/notebook file. You can then visit each setting by going on to a new flipchart/notebook file page or document and annotate text as you wish, e.g. vocabulary about place. Children can then create work based on these texts.

2 Create texts that present dialogue in stories using features like statements, questions, exclamations, paragraphing. Place these on a flipchart/notebook and highlight where dialogue occurs.

4 & 5 Display playscripts on the IWB and annotate them to show the differences between them and prose, e.g. stage directions. You can model this and the children then work away from the board on related work. Alternatively, a group could work at the board annotating a playscript by themselves and presenting it to the rest of the class later.

6 Read poems from the IWB using CD-ROMs, typed text or copied text (e.g. from government resources) or the Internet. You can then study words and phrases that create impact by selecting and highlighting them.

7 Display rhyming and non-rhyming poetry on a flipchart and compare layouts and impact. Model this on the board and annotate or highlight as appropriate. The Internet is a good source of poems for this purpose.

8 Identify keywords to express viewpoints by highlighting them in a displayed text.

Writing composition

9 Brainstorm (text boxes or Kidspiration by Tag Learning or SMART Ideas) on a given topic. Get the children to brainstorm ideas on the IWB with you as the scribe, or let a group of them work on their own or supported by a teaching assistant.

10 Ask the children to create their own passages of dialogue on a flipchart, based on what they have been reading. This can be modelled by you or done by small groups. It would be useful if the work could be word processed away from the board so it can be displayed on the IWB and discussed.

11 On the IWB, write a description of a setting in the style of a familiar story.

Collect sentences and phrases for story openings and endings and revisit them periodically via a stored flipchart. There are lots of resources that can be obtained from **www.sutton.lincs.sch.uk/pages/zone/story/start.html**.

12 Create a flipchart/notebook file dictionary of words and phrases that the children can use to write their own poems and short descriptions.

13 Model and create calligrams on the IWB and then let groups of children work out their own on the IWB.

14 Model the creation of a simple playscript on the IWB. Children will have to create their own away from the board.

15 Model how to paragraph work by using the highlighter tool to summarise information from a text. Get the children to come out to the board and, in small groups, write a paragraph including dialogue.

Non-fiction

Reading comprehension

16 Place the words 'non-fiction', 'fiction' and 'fact' on the board and match them to given meanings. Model examples on the board and then save the flipchart. You could scan in book covers to give a visual idea of fiction and non-fiction books.

17 Display both fiction and non-fiction texts on the IWB and compare styles and structures. Annotate and highlight as appropriate.

18 Create a flipchart/notebook file to compare how information is organised using contents, indexes, headings, sub-headings, etc. Annotate and highlight as appropriate. The use of a document camera might be appropriate here.

19 Analyse texts, underlining key words and phrases with the pen or highlighter tool (see Figure 13). Analyse ICT text in this fashion.

20 Display information text on the IWB and then highlight parts of it to get the overall meaning.

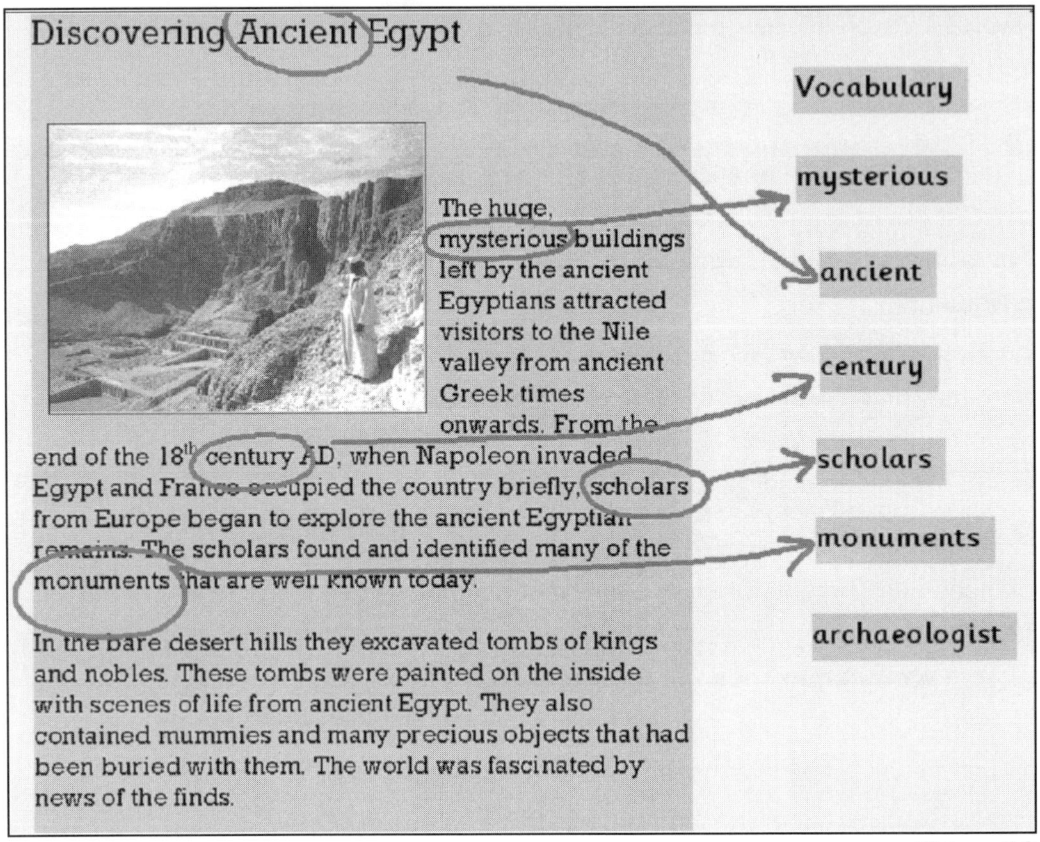

Figure 13

Writing composition

21 Display different sources of information and model making a single record from them. The highlighter or pen tool could be used to good effect here. You would need to use several pages on the IWB to scroll through the different texts.

22 Write a non-chronological report for a defined audience, e.g. other pupils, parents. Model the writing on the IWB and then groups of children create their flipchart version. Not all children will work at the board, but a rota system could be used.

Term 2 Text level work

Fiction and Poetry

Reading comprehension

1 Collect examples of traditional story language and display them on a flipchart, e.g. now, when, a long time ago. Children can come up to the IWB to write or say what happens next. This could also be a group activity at the board.

2 Collect story themes and display them on the IWB (short extracts). Produce a set of phrases that can then be matched to the text using the select tool.

3 Discuss characters and their views. Present characters in different ways, e.g. posters, letters, diagrams. Create examples of these on a flipchart/notebook file and use them as a starting point for discussion or writing.

4 Read out a poem projected onto the board. Annotate and highlight as appropriate.

Writing composition

6 Create a flipchart/notebook file outlining the main points of stories (p.34 of the NLS handbook). The children can come out to the IWB and annotate keywords (or use the highlighter pen) as directed.

7 Write out jumbled-up incidents from a story and use the select tool to re-sequence them. Use a flipchart page with a templated flow chart to link story elements. You could use images that tell a story and then rearrange them.

8 Create different ways of presenting a character on a flipchart/notebook file, e.g. an image, a labelled diagram, a letter, a flow chart and use this as a starting point for the children to write a character portrait. Using SMART Ideas would be useful here, as each heading you create can lead you to a different starting point for writing about character.

9 Create a template on a flipchart to write out a story idea based on an existing myth or fable but with the children making new characters and settings. The children could write on the board, work orally or you could act as scribe. A group of children could do this when working independently.

10 Read out a series of story endings for traditional stories and then model different endings on the IWB. Write out typical phrases and expressions.

11 The same as number 10, but use poetry as the text and create new verses instead of endings.

Non-fiction

Reading comprehension

12–14 Create flipcharts/notebook files on instructional texts (recipes, bullets, keys, etc) and then use them as the base for questioning on the purpose (12), merits (13) and organisation (14) of the said text. You may want to scan these texts to save time.

15 Display instructions on the IWB for the children to follow. Annotate as appropriate.

Writing composition

16 Get a group of children to work at the IWB to write or type out instructions. You could model this first. If other groups have a computer available they could word process their instructions, save their work, load it onto the machine operating the IWB and demonstrate it to the whole class, and perhaps get them to follow their own instructions.

17 Make notes by showing the children, on the IWB, how to highlight keywords in text and work in shortened forms, using flowcharts as created on the IWB or using an application called Kidspiration or SMART Ideas (p.35 of the NLS handbook has more detail).

Term 3 Text level work

Fiction and Poetry

Reading comprehension

1 Create the main points of stories in short form (a few separate sentences) on a flipchart and mix them up. Get the children to re-sequence them using the select tool. Do this for more than one story and save them so you can compare them (could be done orally or as a written exercise).

2 Create a short text and analyse it, e.g. a story start or a descriptive text, with the children highlighting adjectives for description.

3 Change a short piece of work from the 1st person to the 3rd person by annotating over the relevant words to change them.

4 Compare real-life recounts and fiction by having both types of text on a flipchart or saved Internet page and annotating as desired. If you have Adobe Acrobat software (not the reader) you can save pages for later use and annotation.

5 Create texts on a flipchart/notebook file that show a character's feelings and then highlight relevant sections.

6 Put some calligrams, nonsense poems and absurdities onto a flipchart/notebook file and read, model and discuss them using the pen or highlighter tool. There are lots of humorous poems on **www.gigglepoetry.com/poetryfun.cfm**.

7 Display poems on a flipchart/notebook file or via the Internet or CD-ROM and annotate rhyme, alliteration and other effects.

8 Consider works by the same author. Create a flipchart anthology of work for display and comparison, especially the characters in different books.

Writing composition

10 Plan a sequence of episodes modelled on a known story (in the correct sequence). Use a flow chart or writing frame displayed on a big screen and complete it as a class or group (see Figure 14).

11 Write openings to stories that have tension, mood or scene setting. Annotate and highlight as appropriate. Get the children to create their own openings – display appropriate word lists on the IWB that the children have to use in creating or completing a given text. One group can work at the IWB. If other groups have a computer available, they could word process their openings, save their work, load it onto the machine operating the IWB and demonstrate it to the whole class.

12 Write a 3rd person account. Alter sentences on a flipchart changing from the 3rd to 1st person by annotation.

14 Use 4Books (created by the 2Simple software company) to model creating a book review, but use the IWB. This piece of software allows for the modelling of a book review on a large screen.

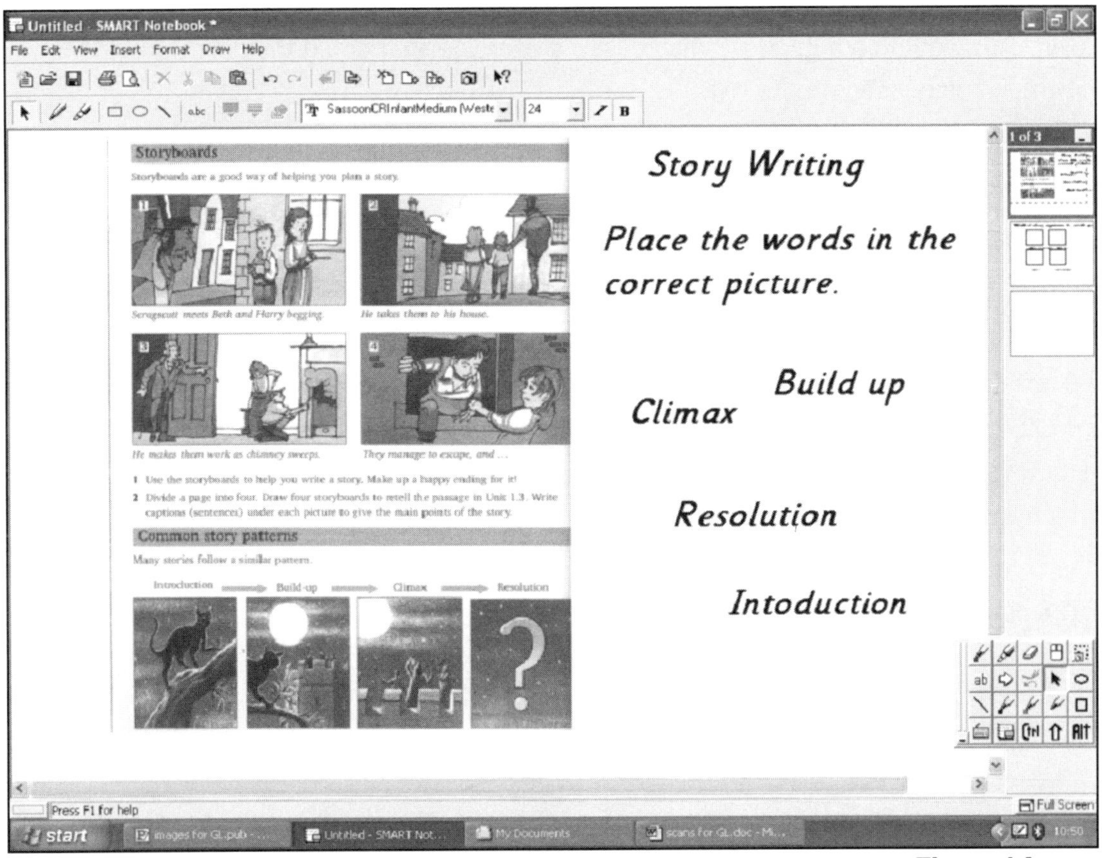

Figure 14

15 Create a poem template on an IWB flipchart or a Word document, with a word bank that uses onomatopoeic words to create sound effects. Use alliteration, too. It would be useful here to link the words to sound files for greater effect (Promethean board users only). SMART users will have to use the hyperlink page.

Non-fiction

Reading comprehension

16 Create a range of letters on a flipchart/notebook file or a Word document and display them on the IWB. Ask the children to identify what kind of letter they are reading, e.g. a recount, a letter of complaint, an enquiry letter.

17 Create an index and locate information from it. Use the highlighter or pen tool. You could use the Internet for this task.

19 Present a text on the IWB and ask the children to do an oral summary. This can be done as a class or group. Keywords could be highlighted first.

Year 3

Writing composition

20 Create messages on a flipchart/notebook file, with the teacher modelling or as a group, e.g. create messages linked to work in other subjects. Show examples on a flipchart/notebook file and then ask the children to create their own. This would be a good word-processing exercise that could then be shown and discussed on the IWB.

21 Show a page created in Word and displayed on the IWB, then annotate and control it to show layouts and fonts. Alternatively, annotate over a 'live' Word page.

22 Use a flipchart/notebook file to experiment in recounting an event in a variety of ways, e.g. story, letter, report. Create an example of each on a separate flipchart page and then get the children to create work from there.

23 Write a letter that has mixed up paragraphs and use the select tool to put the paragraphs in the correct order.

25 Model how to make notes on a flipchart/notebook page by revising shorthand forms of words.

26 Practise note taking by asking a group of children to make notes on a given text. They could highlight key sentences and then rewrite them as a summary

Year 4

Term 1 Word level work

Revision and consolidation from Year 3

1 Identify phonemes in speech and writing.

- On the IWB, highlight phonemes in words with the highlighter or pen tool.
- Use the select tool to blend the phonemes together to complete a word. You will need to create words that are split according to their phonemes for this activity.
- Look at the high-frequency lists from KS1 and Year 3. Read them out and discuss. Display these on the IWB.
- Display a multi-syllabic word on the board and highlight the syllables using the highlighter tool.
- Display unfamiliar text on the IWB and read through it with the children. Question the text by using spelling or phonic knowledge as a cue. Use the highlighter or pen tool as appropriate.

Spelling strategies

2 Keep a list of words that children get wrong continuously, then put them on the IWB. Practise breaking them up syllabically, so that the children learn them.

3 Use independent spelling strategies.

- Display words on the IWB, read them out and highlight the phonemes.
- Recognise common letter strings by highlighting them with the highlighter tool. Build words from the roots of a main word, e.g. 'medical', 'medicine'. Use the pen tool for this.
- Spell by analogy, e.g. 'light', 'fright', 'sight'. Write letters on the IWB and add them to 'ight' to make new words. Use the select tool for this.
- Create a word bank to be displayed on the IWB and use it to help write sentences. Third-party word processors like Granada Writer or Textease (Studio) are ideal for this purpose. Display work via the IWB. Use the *Cambridge Learner's Dictionary* by Granada Learning to investigate dictionary work on the IWB.

4 Write new spellings on the IWB or in Granada Writer/Textease and make sure they are in a column. Use the curtain tool to reveal them in turn. Alternatively, write them out, say the word, rub it out and ask a child to spell it on the board. If you use Textease, you can use a mouse-over function, where you pass a mouse over a word and it disappears for a set amount of time, then reappears.

Spelling conventions and rules

5 Display two-syllable words containing double consonants on the IWB and highlight appropriately. Use the select tool to add 'le' to the ends of words. Alternatively, use the pen tool.

6 Distinguish between the spellings and meanings of homophones, e.g. 'to', 'two' and 'too'. Display sentences on the IWB and ask the children to add one of those three. Add to them using the select or pen tool.

7 Display words on the IWB and add verb endings like 's', 'ed' and 'ing', using the select tool.

8 Spell irregular tense changes, e.g. 'go', 'went' and 'could'. Do this by creating sentences with the words missing and asking the children to use the select tool to drag the correct version into the sentence. Alternatively, use the pen tool.

9 Display a selection of words on the IWB and use the select tool to add the suffixes 'al', 'ary', 'ic', 'ship', 'hood', 'ness' and 'ment'. You will need to use the text tool for this or an application like Granada Writer or Textease.

10 Display parts of the words in Appendix List 2 of the NLS handbook and use the select tool to join them together. You could also ask the children to look, say, cover and spell them on a new page. The children could come out to the board and write these spellings into a sentence. You could model this and then bring a group out to work on their own.

Vocabulary extension

11 Display words on the IWB and ask the children to give meanings for these words orally. Alternatively, have a selection of meanings on the board and the children use the select tool to associate the correct meaning with the word.

12 Display lists of words that have similar beginnings and place them in alphabetical order according to the third and fourth place letters, using the select tool.

13 Display a word list of rhyming words and get the children to use this to compose a jingle. Model this at the board and then invite a group to work on the IWB in the time allocated to individual work.

14 Display nouns and adjectives such as 'fix', 'simple', 'solid', 'comment' and 'just' and make them into verbs by adding the suffixes 'ate' and 'ify'. Use the select tool to join them.

Handwriting

Use a flipchart/notebook page with lines on it for the children to practise showing a neat, clear hand that has correct sizes of ascenders and descenders, and make sure that the proportions of the letters are correct (see Figure 15).

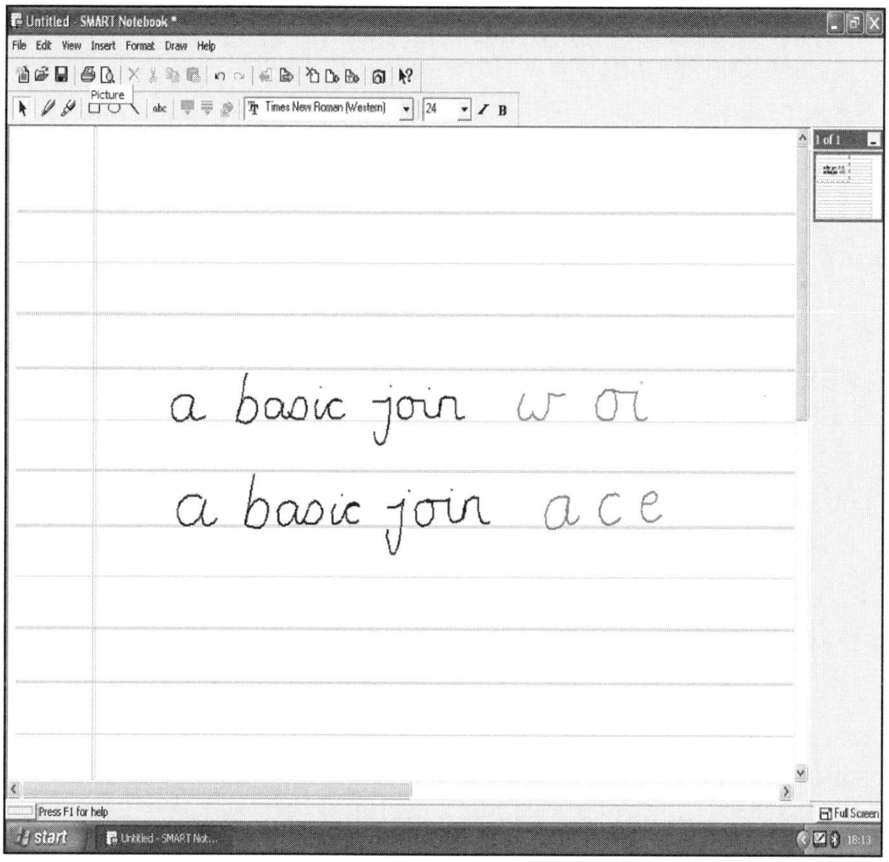

Figure 15

Term 2 Word level work

Spelling and vocabulary revision and consolidation from Year 3 is as per the first term for both the revision and the spelling strategies.

Spelling conventions and rules

5 Investigate what happens to words ending in 'f' when a suffix is added. Write words ending in 'f' on the IWB. The children will use the select tool to append the suffix to the word. They have to find out what happens to the 'f'. Use the pen tool to help when adding the suffixes.

6 Spell words with the common ending 'ight'. Display lots of letters on the board and have 'ight' written on another part of the board. Use the select tool to match them up.

7 Recognise and spell the prefix 'al'. Use the same method as above – prefixes are displayed on the board and then moved to words using the select tool.

8 Display words from Appendix List 2 of the NLS handbook on the IWB. Ask the children to read them and define their meanings. Then, on a blank flipchart or page, invite them to come out and spell a few of them.

Vocabulary extension

9 Display a short piece of text on the IWB. Ask the children to use the select tool to add words that are more accurate or interesting than some of the common choices that would normally be available, e.g. words that are an alternative to 'got' or 'nice' or 'good'. Children will need to use the pen tool for this activity.

10 Look at gender with the suffix 'ess'. Have a word displayed on the IWB, e.g. 'prince', and get the children to use the select tool to add 'ess' to make 'princess'. Adjustments in spelling will have to be made using the pen tool. Look at exceptions such as fox/vixen, king/queen and invite the children to match them together using the select tool. Adding images will enhance the work and provide visual prompts.

11 Explain that vocabulary changes over time. Have a collection of words on screen with the old meanings, e.g. 'wireless' changes to 'transistor', which changes to 'radio'. Ask the children to select them and group them together. Images relating to the words would go down well here.

12 Get the children to define a familiar word. Model this on the IWB. First of all define the word using four words, then see if the children can eliminate any of those words to make the meaning more concise. (Do a meaning with four, then three, then two words.) Annotate work as required.

13 Explore a range of suffixes that can be added to nouns and verbs to make adjectives. For example, using the IWB, you would have the words 'wash' on one side and 'able' on another, 'hope' and 'ful', 'shock' and 'ing' and use the select tool to match them up.

Handwriting

Handwriting is as for the first term. Make sure that sizes and proportions are correct. Have lines displayed on the IWB and get the children to write in the correct size, using proper spacing.

Term 3 Word level work

Spelling and vocabulary revision and consolidation from Year 3 is as per the first term for both the revision and the spelling strategies.

Spelling conventions and rules

5 Display words on the IWB and get the children to highlight certain letter strings, e.g. 'wa' in 'water' and 'wash', or 'wo' in 'worship' or 'won'. Ask the children to deduce the meaning of the words.

6 Get the children to identify words on the IWB with different pronunciations but with common letter strings, e.g. tough, through, plough. Ask the children to highlight the letter string and say the different pronunciations.

7 Write some word roots on the IWB and have words displayed on the board in a random order that need to be listed under these headings, e.g. root – 'vent', related words – 'invent', 'prevent'; root – 'press', related words – 'pressure', 'depress', and so on. The teacher could then investigate the origins and meanings of the words.

8 Practise extending and compounding words by adding parts like 'ful' or 'ly', 'ive', ition' or 'ist'. You might have the word 'event' written on one side of the board and 'ful' on the other. You would then use the select tool to join them together.

9 A similar activity would be to have words in a random order placed on the IWB, with the suffixes 'ible', 'able', 'ive' and 'tion' next to them. You would then use the select tool to join them together.

10 Distinguish between the possessive form of 'its', and the contracted form 'it's'. Have a sentence or sentences with spaces where 'its' or 'it's' need to be inserted. Ask the children to use the select tool to add them in. You could also use the pen tool.

Vocabulary extension

11 Investigate compound words. Create words on different parts of the IWB that together make a compound word, e.g. 'hand' and 'bag'. Use the select tool to join them together, e.g. to make 'handbag'.

12 Explain how diminutives are formed, e.g. using the suffix 'est' or the prefix 'mini'. Create a list of words on the IWB and add 'est' or 'mini' with the select tool to the words to make them diminutive.

Handwriting

Use the IWB with lines on and invite the children to come out and write text on the board. Check on sizes, heights and distances from each word.

Term 1 Sentence level work

Grammatical awareness

1 Ask children to load saved work onto the computer that controls the IWB and do a collective check on the work. It might be better if a group's work is looked at first to avoid any individual upset if lots of errors are spotted. Alternatively, a group could self-check their own work at the IWB.

2 Revise work on verbs by looking at some text in the past tense and ask the children to highlight the verbs that indicate that it is. Also, display text on the IWB and ask the children if they can change the tense of the verbs using the pen tool. If they can, that means it's a verb.

3 Use cloze procedure for working with 'powerful' verbs. Display a text on the IWB with spaces next to the verbs, and ask the children to use the select tool to add alternative meanings for a verb from a word list, for example

'went' could be replaced by a stronger verb like 'hobbled'. Cricksoft's ClozePro would be useful here.

4 Identify adverbs and understand their functions.

- Place some text on the IWB. Ask the children to highlight any adverbs and note any common endings (e.g. words ending in 'ly').
- When they have highlighted the adverbs, point out to the children where these occur and what they usually help to qualify, i.e. they help to qualify a verb.
- Display a collection of adverbs on the IWB for children to use in the form of a word list, e.g. swiftly, rapidly, sluggishly, brilliantly, dimly, and so on.
- On another page, create text with sentences that have an adverb missing, e.g. 'They left the house ...ly.' The children have to use the pen tool to write in an adverb to complete the sentence.

Sentence construction and punctuation

5 Create a piece of text on the IWB with missing commas and ask the children to add in the commas.

Term 2 Sentence level work

Grammatical awareness

1 Revise work on adjectives and link the work to expressive and figurative language in stories and poetry.

- Examine comparative and superlative adjectives, e.g. 'good', 'better', 'best'. Create some text where these can be inserted using the select tool so the sentences make sense. Also, create a piece of text and compare adjectives on a scale of intensity. For example, you could have some text saying 'The water was...', and the alternatives could be 'hot', 'warm', 'tepid' and 'lukewarm'. Ask the children to drag text from a word list to complete the sentence. This activity could also be created in Granada Writer or Textease.
- On the IWB, write some adjectives on one side of the page and suffixes such as 'ish', 'er' and 'est' on the other. Ask the children to add these to the adjectives using the select tool. Elicit the response relating to degrees of intensity, e.g. warm – warmish, warmer or warmest.
- Relate adjectives to adverbs that indicate degrees of intensity. For example, write words like 'very', 'more' and 'most' on one side of the IWB and a list of adjectives on the other. Link the adverb to the adjective, e.g. 'very' – 'very warm', 'most' – 'most warm', and so on.

Sentence construction and punctuation

2 Use the apostrophe to mark possession.

Display some text with possessive apostrophes omitted and ask the children to come out with a pen and annotate where they should be. Recap the basic rules of apostrophising a singular noun ('the cat' – 'the cat's tail') and a plural noun where the apostrophe comes after the 's' ('the cats' – 'the cats' tails'). Distinguish between the apostrophe for contraction and the apostrophe for possession. Display some text that has both of these missing and get the children to put apostrophes in appropriately. Use the pen tool.

3 Have some sentences displayed on the IWB which, with the select tool, can be reordered and still make sense. Have some sentences that can't be reordered by changing the word order, and have some sentences that might need something adding to them to make sense of the reordering. You will need to create each word separately so it can be moved individually.

4 Have some text displayed on the IWB and ask the children to add commas or any missing connectives and full stops. They could start by simply annotating text with commas and connectives so they are aware of and recognise them.

Term 3 Sentence level work

Grammatical awareness

1 Display text on the IWB that shows verb endings, comparative endings and pluralisation. Model how these are important clues for identifying word classes. You could use the highlighter or pen tool for this.

Sentence construction and punctuation

2 Display text on the IWB with commas, semicolons, hyphens, dashes and speech marks missing, and ask the children to put them in using the pen tool.

3 Explain how the grammar of a sentence alters when the sentence type is altered. For example, change statements to questions and questions to statements. You could write some statements on one side of the board and corresponding questions on the other. These can then be matched up using the select tool. You could also create a positive statement and match it with a negative statement, e.g. 'I am well', 'I am unwell' and notice how they are done. Use the select tool for this (see Figure 16).

4 Use connectives to structure an argument. On the IWB, display the words 'if', 'then', 'on the other hand', 'finally' and 'saw' and ask the children to put them into some text that you have already written out. Use this as a template for structuring an argument and ask the children to create their own. A group could do this collectively at the IWB.

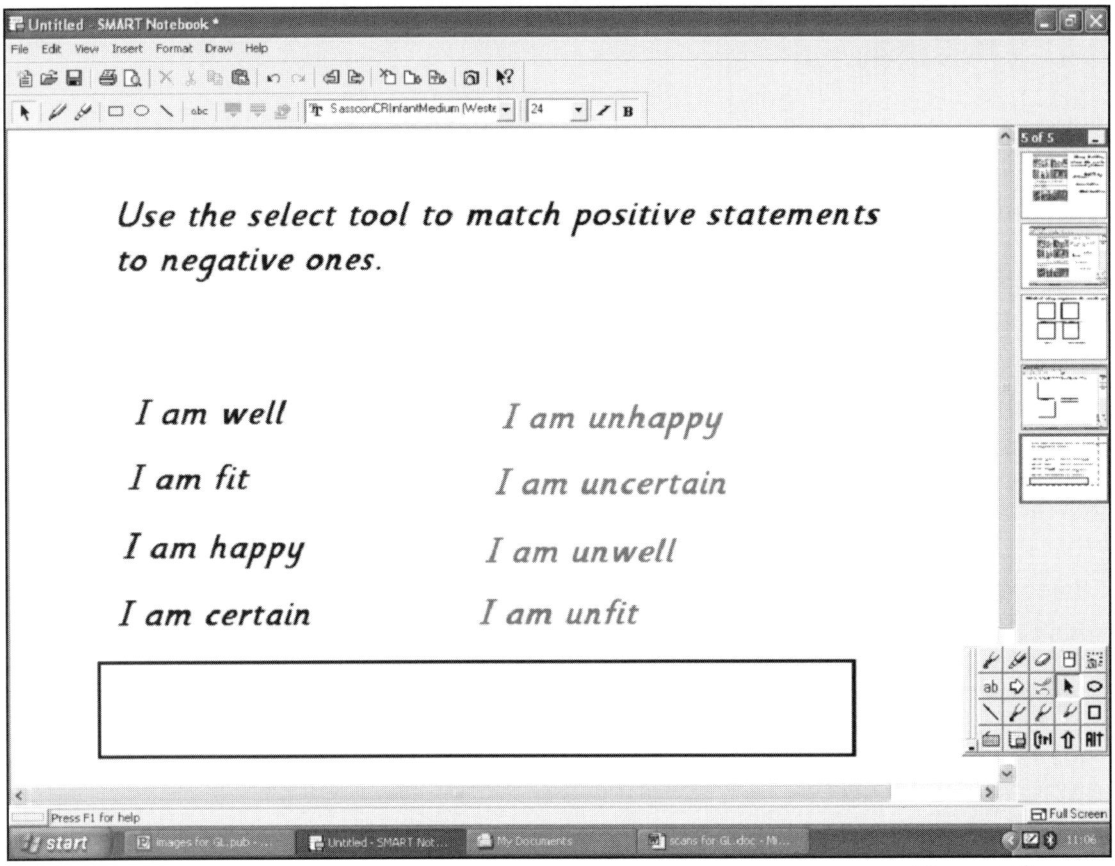

Figure 16

Term 1 Text level work

Fiction and Poetry

Reading comprehension

1 Investigate how settings and characters are built up from small details and how a reader responds to them. On the IWB, have a description of a setting or character. Get children to highlight bits of the text to show how the descriptions of the setting and the character are brought to life by the use of these details.

2 Identify the main characteristics of key characters. You need some text related to a key character displayed on the IWB. The children have to highlight and annotate text that shows what this character is like. Then, with you modelling, they predict what this character might do.

3 On the IWB, display various extracts from a story, related to the passage of time. Get the children to come out and annotate or highlight the parts of the text which show that they know how much time passes in the course of a story.

4 Use the IWB to go through the various stages of storytelling, i.e. how they are started, how setting is created, characters are introduced, build-ups are organised, conflicts are detailed and resolutions are arrived at. This can be done very well using a flowchart technique, where you draw a box and the children make up a story start. (SMART Ideas would work well here.) They can also make

up some characters by coming out and writing about them or writing a keyword about them. This would be an ideal activity away from the IWB, but with groups of children coming back to it to show what they have done. Work would need to be word processed, saved and loaded onto the computer controlling the IWB. Using Kidspiration by Tag Learning could be a useful option here.

5 Ask the children to create a playscript, or use one that you have, and display it on the IWB. The children then read it and note down how it is organised so that they can then perform it. Look at how the settings are indicated – ask the children to come out and highlight the parts of the playscript that show this.

6 Chart the build-up of a play scene – how the scene starts, how the dialogue is expressed, how the scene is concluded. Display a playscript and either you highlight the relevant parts, or invite the children to come out and do it.

7 Compare and contrast poems about similar themes. Display poems by two different authors on the same theme. Highlight things like language, rhymes and so on, and elicit a personal response and preference to them from the children.

8 Use the Internet, with you modelling, to find out about popular authors. Ask the children to come out and highlight sections of information that they find about their favourite authors. Use the pen or highlighter tool, as necessary. Visiting **www.storiesfromtheweb.org** will give you resources about authors.

Writing composition

9 Use the IWB to plan a story. You could have whole-class brainstorming, and you could use flowcharts or diagrams, with the children coming out and

using the IWB. The children could also come out in groups and construct their own plans on the IWB.

10 Acting as a model, plan a story by simply writing notes on the IWB relating the various stages of its telling. What story start are we going to use? What characters are going to be involved? What setting will be described? Ask your children to begin to do any scribing.

11 Write a character sketch. Obtain an image of a character and put it on the IWB screen. Annotate various parts of the physical aspects of the character and, on another flipchart page, write what the character is like. You could display text that describes the character and the children could come out and highlight the main points, then write a sentence about that character themselves.

12 This relates to empathising with situations in historical stories. You could read a story to the children about a character in history and get them to come out and write on the board what they would do if they were in that person's shoes. You could have a pre-prepared text that is already highlighted in case some children have difficulty in empathising.

13 The children write playscripts, for example based on stories they already know. You could display half-completed texts on the IWB and get the children to complete them, with you acting as scribe.

14 The children write poems based on personal or imagined experiences. On the IWB, collect vocabulary, phrases and words suggested by the children, then ask them to write the poems themselves in a cooperative manner, with one group creating the poem on the IWB.

15 Explain the use of paragraphs in story writing. Create a text on the IWB that has no paragraphs, then ask the children to highlight where paragraphs could be placed.

Non-fiction

Reading comprehension

16 Display different kinds of texts on the IWB and elicit from the children an awareness of the different styles, content, structure and layout. Annotate and control as appropriate.

17 Identify the features of non-fiction text. Display a non-fiction text on the IWB and identify features like headings, lists, bullets, etc. using the highlighter and the annotation tool, so that the children can gain sufficient information about that text.

18 The children select opening sentences that set the scene. Create extracts of texts on different flipchart pages or in different pages of Word and get the children to come out and highlight the key phrases and keywords that convey information in the opening sentences.

19 Display text on the IWB that is related to what is fact and what is opinion. Ask the children to highlight one or the other to show that they recognise the difference.

20 Scan a section of a newspaper or obtain on web page of one so that you can display the layout of a newspaper on the IWB and discuss how it's broken up. Using a document camera would be useful here.

21 On the IWB, have two or three headlines written out and get the children to work collaboratively in groups to predict and make up a newspaper story. On a new flipchart/notebook page, ask the children to come out and use a flow diagram to tell you about the story. Display the original story if possible to compare versions. Alternatively, they could do this orally.

22 Display an instructional text on the IWB. Highlight and identify the various aspects of the text, e.g. the use of imperative verbs – 'do this', 'cut this', 'open this'.

23 Display ICT texts and illustrate their various properties. Display Word, for example, and demonstrate how you can scroll the text up and down, showing its linear structure. Show how some texts can be non-linear, e.g. PowerPoint where you can jump from one idea to the other. Show how you might incorporate sound into Word. You could also use Granada Writer/Textease for this purpose. Use the mouse function, pen and highlighter tool for this exercise.

Writing composition

24 This would be a group activity on the IWB. A group of children creates a newspaper story based on a headline. They would first do a draft, writing in the text and laying it out. Then they would edit the draft, organising and writing paragraphs and giving a presentation to the class about what they have done. Other groups could use a saved Word document to show their work on the IWB.

25 Challenge the class to create instructions on how to do something, e.g. how to operate a video player, and give a group the opportunity to use the IWB. They should all create a list of instructions that they can tell to the rest of the class. One group works at the IWB while the others work in groups on computers away from the IWB and visit it later.

26 Display some written instructions on the IWB that need sub-headings or numbering, and ask the children to put these in or order the text correctly (see Figure 17). After modelling this, children could work at computers on different texts, putting in headings, etc. Any work created could be loaded onto the machine working the IWB and offered to the class for discussion. This would be excellent for collaborative work.

27 The children could work in a group at the IWB to write a non-chronological report.

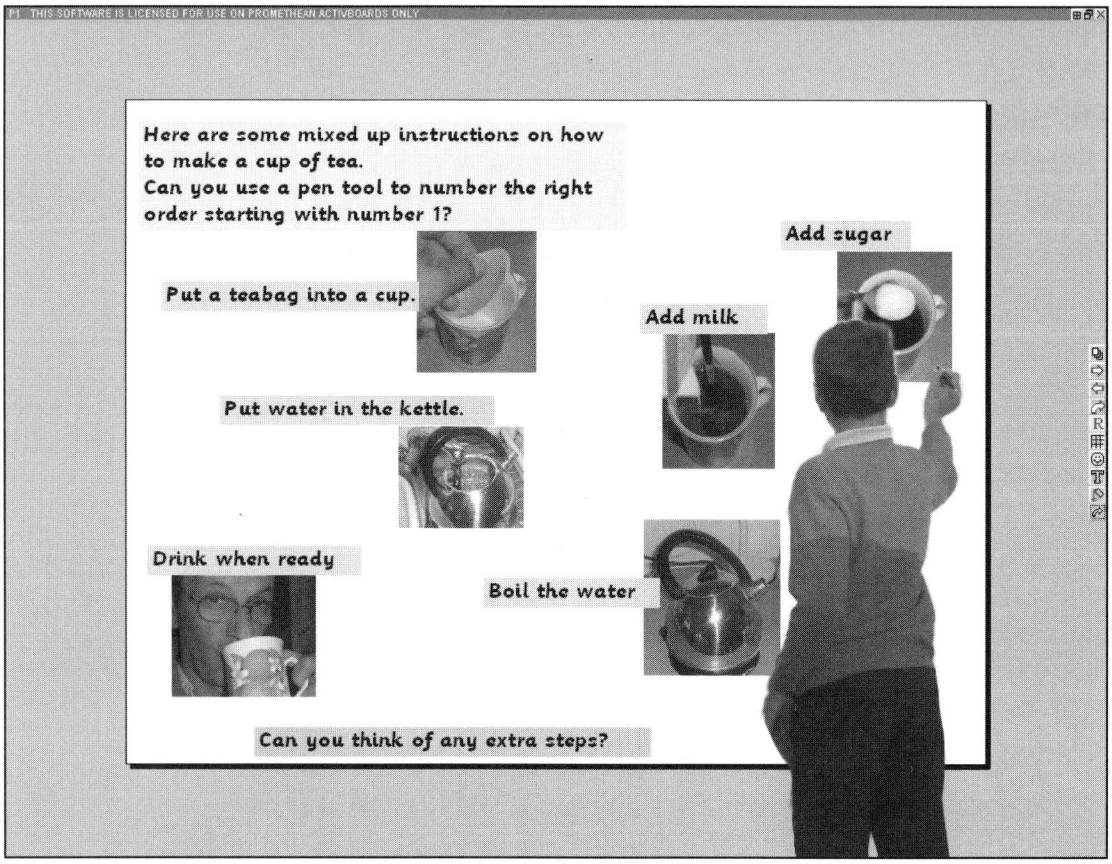

Figure 17

Term 2 Text level work

Fiction and Poetry

Reading comprehension

1 Understand how writers create imaginary worlds such as science fiction. Get the children to highlight details of settings related to a planet or imaginary world in text displayed on the IWB. You could use images captured from the Internet to act as a stimulus.

2 Display a similar text on the IWB and get the children to annotate various parts of the text related to setting. Discuss how the setting will influence the characters' behaviour.

3 On the IWB, have three or four texts with different settings across a range of different stories. Read these and then model how you would evaluate them. Compare them with each other.

4 On the IWB, have text containing either expressive or descriptive language. Invite the children to highlight various phrases and words that show mood, expectation, or emotion.

5 Display a poem or some prose on the IWB and get the children to highlight or annotate the figurative language, e.g. the use of similes.

6 Display a poem on the IWB and get the children to highlight words that they think make the poem sound old, e.g. archaic words.

7 Display a poem on the IWB and get the children to annotate or highlight rhyming patterns in the verses. As a class group, ask the children to read these out.

8 Collect some stories of different genres. Scan their covers into a flipchart or onto a PowerPoint slide and display them on the IWB. Talk about the authors, the themes and how they've used them, for example you could look at horror books or adventure books.

9 Display different kinds of texts on the IWB and ask the children what the intended audience is. Is it for five year olds, adults, junior children?

Writing composition

10 Create a piece of text on the IWB that has spaces for missing text or cloze procedure, and get the children to insert adjectives and figurative language into the text.

11 On the IWB, have a template for a poem based on a style of a poet you have discussed, and get the children to add archaic expressions, similes, and so on using the select or pen tool. Words can be created or come from a word list.

12 Invite a group of children to come to the IWB and write a story for a chapter with a particular audience in mind. Use either IWB software or a word processor.

13 Display some descriptive writing on the IWB and use it as a starter for children to write their own examples of descriptive or expressive language. They could use adjectives and similes you have created in a word list. Alternately, create a piece of text with spaces for similes and adjectives to be put in – the children can use the select tool to insert words/phrases from a word list.

14 With you acting as scribe, use the IWB to edit a sentence or passage. Invite the children to suggest words that can be deleted – words that aren't important or are repeated – so that the text is edited down. You could either edit the text or rewrite the sentence using the pen tool.

Non-fiction

Reading comprehension

15 Scan in the covers, headings and contents pages of a non-fiction book and display them on the IWB. Get the children to appraise what kind of book it is.

16 Create a flipchart or notebook file on a given topic, outlining how the children might find information on it.

17 Ask the children to highlight key words and phrases in a text relating to a certain subject so that they can later summarise that text. Alternatively, a group of children can write a summary on a new flipchart page.

18 Create text on an IWB and ask the children to highlight or mark with a pen tool the key words and sentences.

19 Display text on the IWB the paragraphs of which are mixed up. Ask the children to reorder these paragraphs to make a correct sequence, using the select tool. They could number them using the pen tool if selecting is awkward due to the size of a paragraph. It might be useful to use Word here to select and move text around, but display it on the big screen.

20 Use an IWB to display explanatory text and highlight/annotate key features:

- purpose
- structure
- language
- presentation.

Writing composition

21 Model how to make short notes. Discuss a text on the IWB, highlighter various key words and phrases. In the space beneath the text, demonstrate to the children how to abbreviate these ideas. Get the children to write them down in their books or, alternatively, they can work as a group on a new flipchart page, coming out and making short notes on it.

22 Display text in note form on the IWB and elicit from the children how to make connected prose from that piece of text. You will have to model this process. The children can give oral explanations and you can act as scribe.

23 Collect information from lots of sources and model how to present it in a simple format. Use a flowchart or a labelled diagram. You could have extracts of the sources in pre-written form and get the children to use the select tool to put them in the correct order.

24 Teach the children how to paragraph using coloured pens on an IWB. Use green for an introductory sentence, orange for the contents part of the paragraph and red for an end sentence. Discuss and model features like headings and numbering.

25 Get the children to use the select tool on the IWB to sequence a process, e.g. making a cup of tea, how to make toast. The children use the select tool to put everything in the right order.

Term 3 Text level work

Fiction and Poetry

Reading comprehension

1 Display text on the IWB and get the children to highlight words, phrases and sentences that show social, moral or cultural issues. Discuss with the children how characters in the story deal with these issues. Annotate and highlight as necessary.

2 Display short extracts of stories from other cultures on the IWB and get the children to highlight how they are different or similar from their own customs and relationships.

3 Use the IWB to display texts with short paragraphs and model how these paragraphs are used to build up ideas.

4 Display the words 'verse', 'chorus', 'couplet', 'stanza', 'rhyme' and 'rhythm' on one side of an IWB flipchart/notebook file, and have their explanations jumbled up on the other side. Use the select tool to match them up.

5 Display some poetry on the IWB and get the children to annotate syllables in each line. Alternatively, they could clap out and count the syllables.

6 Display a poem on the IWB and highlight any rhyming patterns. Discuss their effect (see Figure 18).

Figure 18

7 Display different forms of poetry on the IWB and identify them, e.g. a skipping song, choruses, and so on.

8 Display text that has a dilemma in it from a story. Use the highlighter tool to mark out the dilemma and ask the children what a possible solution might be. (This could be written down.) From a new flipchart page, read out what the author's solution is.

9 Display extracts of stories and poems by the same author on the IWB. Make comparisons and identify familiar features. Annotate or highlight as necessary.

Writing composition

11 Ask the children to word process a short story about a dilemma and display finished work on the IWB. Ask the children to read out their story and highlight the dilemma they wrote about. Better still, get others to do this.

12 Display an ending for a known story on the IWB and encourage the children to talk about an alternative ending and how it would change the reader's view of the characters in the original story. A group of children could come up and do this on the IWB as a guided session.

13 Give the children some ideas for a story and get them to plan it out on the IWB. This could be done on a flowchart with a group of children. The children would then write out the story.

14 Ask the children to write poems with different styles and structures. Get a group to come out and work together to create a poem on the board to show to the class. This could be done on another computer and then transferred to the IWB computer and displayed.

15 This could be linked in with number 14. Children in a group could delete words from a poem that they have written on the IWB. They could change and experiment with figurative language.

Non-fiction

Reading comprehension

16 Display examples of the following on the IWB: a letter to the press, an article, a discussion of an issue in a book, e.g. about the environment or animal welfare, and evaluate these in class. Annotate or highlight as necessary.

17 Show, via a template on the IWB, how an argument is presented. Annotate as necessary.

18 Display examples of persuasive writing on the IWB and get the children to annotate or highlight words that are used to convince the reader. Then, on a separate flipchart/notebook page, get the children to come out in groups to try to create some persuasive writing on a given topic. Groups of children could word process this work and display results for analysis by the class. If you visit **www.learn.co.uk/glearning/primary/lessons/ks2/lesson1/intro.asp** you'll find resources and ideas focussing on persuasive writing.

19 Create a series of advertisements on the IWB and discuss their appeal. Annotate as necessary.

20 Display a longish sentence or paragraph and get the children to delete or cross out words that are not important, so that they summarise that piece of text.

Writing composition

21 Display a sequence of points out of order on the IWB and get the children to use the select tool to put them back into the correct sequence. This enables them to collect their thoughts together on a given topic.

22 On the IWB, display a writing frame related to persuasive writing. Model how to fill it in with the children. They can then complete their own and, if saved, they can display their work on the IWB and present it.

23 Create a piece of text on the IWB, for example a letter or a report that persuades somebody to do something. Model this and highlight the points and the words that are persuasive. Ask the children to work independently or in groups, from that starting point, to create their own persuasive text. They could word process their work and then display it on the IWB and present their argument.

24 Ask the children to read a text on the IWB, highlight keywords and then write a summary of the text . Alternatively, on the IWB, a group of children can then summarise that text on a new page.

25 Model designing an advertisement, such as a poster or radio jingle, and get the children to work on this. They can come up in groups to the IWB to design their own advertisements. They could use Microsoft Publisher for this and display finished work on the IWB.

Term 1 Word level work

Spelling strategies

1 Display a list of commonly misspelt words on the IWB in their misspelt and correct form, and then show them misspelt in a passage of text. The children can come out to the IWB to annotate over to correct them.

2 On the IWB, display a set of words that the children know, then invite them to come out to the IWB to spell new words from similar patterns. Alternatively, you can use the select tool to match words with similar spelling patterns to an original.

3 Use independent spelling strategies.

- The IWB can be used to build up spelling by highlighting the syllabic parts of words, prefixes, suffixes and common letter strings.
- Build up words from other known words, or identify words from within longer words by using the highlighter tool.
- Use the IWB to show an on-screen dictionary, like the *Cambridge Learner's Dictionary*, to practise using a dictionary. Also use the spell checker in Word.
- Recognise common letter strings by highlighting them. With the children, look at words and say 'Does this look right?' Underline any potential errors using the pen tool.

Spelling conventions and rules

4 Examine the properties in words ending in vowels other than the letter 'e'. On the IWB, display these words and discuss and annotate appropriately.

5 Work on pluralisation by presenting words on the IWB and using the select tool to add endings like 's', 'es', 'ies'. You will need to use the pen tool to add any changes.

6 Collect meanings and spellings of words that have the prefixes 'trans', 'auto', 'bi', 'tele' and 'circum'. On the IWB, have a word without the prefix on one part of the flipchart and the prefix on another part, and use the select tool to join them together (e.g. 'bi' and 'cycle'). Discuss the meanings. You could also match your words to meanings displayed on the IWB (see Figure 19).

Vocabulary extension

7 Have different words of similar meaning and mix these with words that are not synonyms. Separate out the synonyms and sort them according to their meaning, using the select tool. For example, 'angry' is a synonym of 'irritated', 'frustrated' and 'upset'.

Year 5

8 On the IWB, identify word roots. For example, look at the words ‘signature’ and ‘signal’ on the IWB and get the children to highlight the word ‘sign’ as the word root. Another example is ‘bomb’, which is the root of ‘bombastic’ and ‘bombard’.

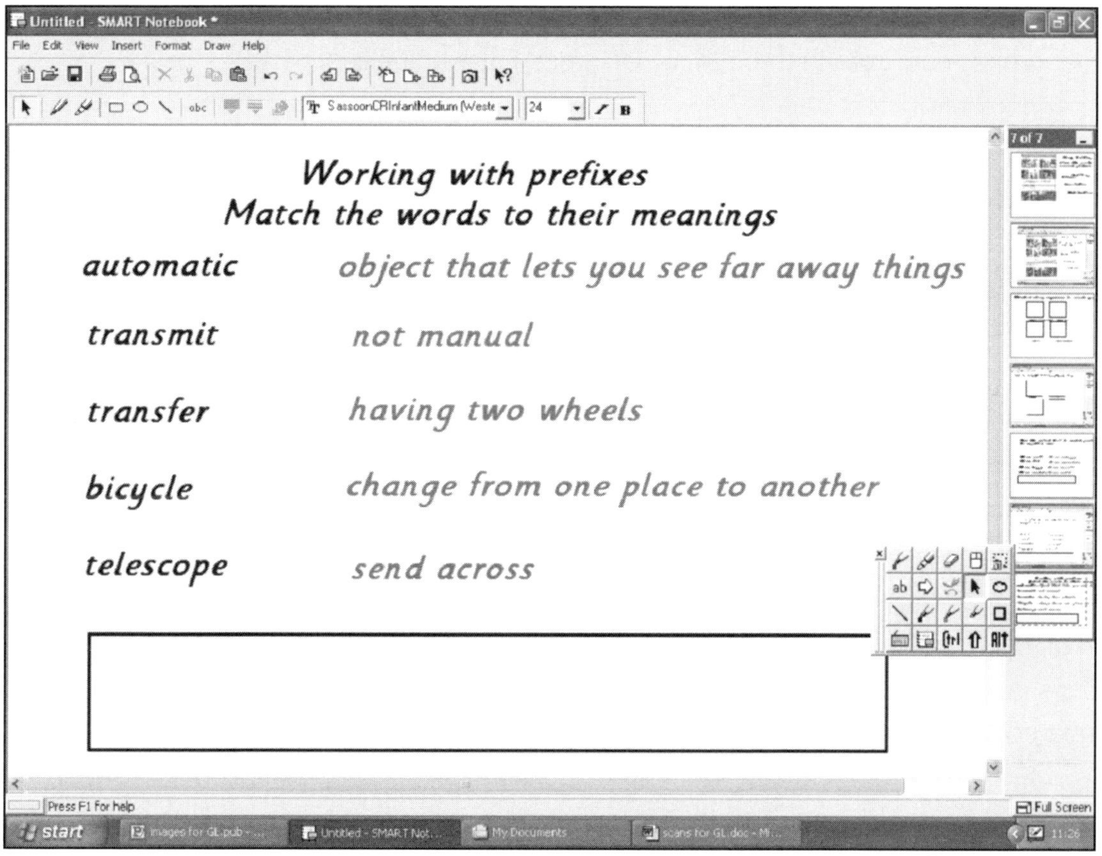

Figure 19

9 Display idioms and some potential meanings mixed up on the board. Ask the children to use the select tool to match the most suitable meaning to the idiom.

10 Display text on the IWB and invite the children to highlight or annotate adverbs that qualify verbs. Alternatively, use cloze procedure relating to adverbs. Use the select tool to add the missing words from a given word list or simply use the pen tool.

Term 2 Word level work

Spelling strategies

Numbers 1–3 are the same as for the previous term.

Spelling conventions and rules

4 Explore spelling patterns of consonants and speculate rules.

- For example, the double ‘l’ in ‘full’ becomes a single ‘l’ when used as a suffix, so you could practise modelling relevant words on the IWB. Use the select tool to join the suffix ‘ful’ to other displayed words, e.g. art/artful, play/playful.

- On the IWB, write words like 'hum' and 'sit' and then add 'ing'. Note how you have to double the consonant. Invite the children to use the select tool to join them up and try to spot where they need to double the consonant. You'll have to use the pen tool to make any adjustments.
- On the IWB, write words like 'circus' and 'accident' and get the children to read them out. Note that the 'c' is soft when followed by an 'i'. Use the pen or highlighter tool for this.

5 On the IWB, write words like 'rough', 'cough' and 'bough'. Use the highlighter tool to show that they have the same letter string, but note that they have different pronunciations. Ask the children if they can write other 'ough' words on the IWB.

6 On the IWB, write words such as 'eight' and 'ate', 'grate' and 'great', 'rain' and 'reign'. Ask the children to pair them up using the select tool, and note that they sound the same but have different spellings. Discuss the different meanings of the words that sound the same. Highlight and annotate as necessary.

7 On the IWB, display possessive pronouns such as 'their' and 'theirs', 'your' and 'yours', 'my' and 'mine'. They should be jumbled up so that they can be joined together to show the children the correct spelling. Place these pronouns into sentences using the select tool or simply write them into gaps in displayed text using the pen tool. Highlight and annotate as necessary.

8 On the IWB, display several words and add the suffix 'cian' to them using the select tool, e.g. music/musician, and see how the spelling changes.

Vocabulary extension

9 On the IWB, compile a list of technical words that the children have collected. Save it so that you can revisit and read the words from time to time.

10 On the IWB, display words and their antonyms (opposites). Include words that have more than one antonym and get the children to talk about them. You could use the select tool to match them up.

11 On the IWB, display onomatopoeic words jumbled up with words that are not onomatopoeic. Separate out the onomatopoeic words using the select tool. The onomatopoeic words can be linked to a sound file so that when selected they say what they sound like. (This is done by linking to a sound file using Promethean software or the voice recognition on Granada Writer/Textease.)

12 On the IWB, display texts containing metaphorical expressions and figures of speech. Get the children to highlight them to recognise them and offer an explanation.

Term 3 Word level work

Spelling strategies

These are the same as for the previous two terms and have already been covered.

Spelling conventions and rules

4 Spell unstressed vowels in polysyllabic words, e.g. company, portable, poisonous, interest, description, carpet, sector, freedom. Display them on the IWB, highlight the unstressed vowels and discuss. You could place them in gaps in a sentence using the select tool.

5 Investigate spelling rules.

- For example, drop the 'e' with adding 'ing'. On the IWB, have words like 'take', and add 'ing' using the select tool. Use the pen tool to demonstrate to the children that they have to cross off the 'e'.
- Put words like 'hope' and 'love' on the IWB and add the suffixes 'ful' or 'ly' to them. Demonstrate that they keep the 'e'.

6 Transform words by applying the following rules and adding the following prefixes or suffixes to them using the select tool on the IWB. Once you have done this, you could match the words to their meanings using the select tool.

- Words ending in 'e' lose the 'e' when adding 'ing'.
- Change tense by adding 'ed'.
- Negation – add 'un', 'im', 'il'.
- Make comparisons by adding 'er', 'est', 'ish'.
- Change verbs to nouns by adding 'ion', 'ism', 'ology'.
- Change nouns to verbs by adding 'ise', 'ify', 'en'.

7 Again, use the select tool on the IWB to match the following prefixes to words: 'in', 'im', 'ir', 'il', 'pro', 'sus'.

Vocabulary extension

8 Identify words that have come from other languages, e.g. bungalow, spaghetti, boutique. Display these words on the IWB so the children can sight-read them. On a new page, put the word over a country on a displayed map to show its origin. On a third page, ask the children to use the select tool to link the word to the country on a displayed map.

9 Collect words on the IWB that vary across dialects. Use the select tool and a chart to classify the words. One word is displayed at the top of a column and words belonging to that family are dragged to that column.

10 Display words on the IWB like 'telephone' and 'aeroplane' and use the highlighter tool to show a shorter version.

12 Use an on-screen dictionary displayed via the IWB (e.g. *Cambridge Learner's Dictionary*) to explore spellings, meanings and derivations.

13 Create a class dictionary on the IWB that can be visited periodically to check that everybody knows the words.

Term 1 Sentence level work

Grammatical awareness

1 Create a sentence ready to be displayed on the IWB to demonstrate the importance of word order. Make sure that each word of the sentence can be moved, then model how that sentence can be shortened. Can any words be deleted? Get the children to use the rub out, edit or select tool to delete a word without losing the overall sense of the meaning. Can the sentence be rearranged with the select tool to reorder the sentence?

2 Gather together, and display on the IWB, a selection of texts with spaces left for the children to add in 'we' or 'I' or 'you' to go with a certain verb (agreement between nouns and verbs).

Display a text that is in the present tense and ask the children to come out and annotate over the verbs so that they are in the past tense (understanding the basic conventions of standard English).

Display a text that has dialect words in and ask the children to highlight these with the highlighter tool and then to replace them with a more standard English word (understanding the basic conventions of standard English). You could annotate with the pen tool or move the word using the select tool.

3 Create some sentences that need to be made more complex by adding in connectives, for example you could have a piece of text with spaces for a connective to be inserted, and the connective could be dragged in using the select tool. For a harder task, create a piece of text and get the children to write over it or annotate where they think a connective could be put in.

4 Display a piece of text on the IWB and model how that text can be rewritten/adapted to suit younger readers. Some complicated words could be deleted and annotated over to produce simpler words. The children could decide by coming up to the board and crossing out words that wouldn't be needed. A group of children could then come up to the IWB and recreate that piece of text for a particular audience, e.g. younger readers (see Figure 20).

5 To demonstrate the difference between direct and reported speech, you could have examples of two similar sentences, e.g. 'She said "I am going."' and 'She said she was going.' and get the children to use the select tool to match them up to the correct aspect of speech. You could also display a text that contains direct speech and reported speech and ask the children to highlight which is which. You could have some direct speech written on

the board and ask the children to rewrite it as reported speech and vice versa – it would probably be best if you modelled this first, or it could be done later with a group of children.

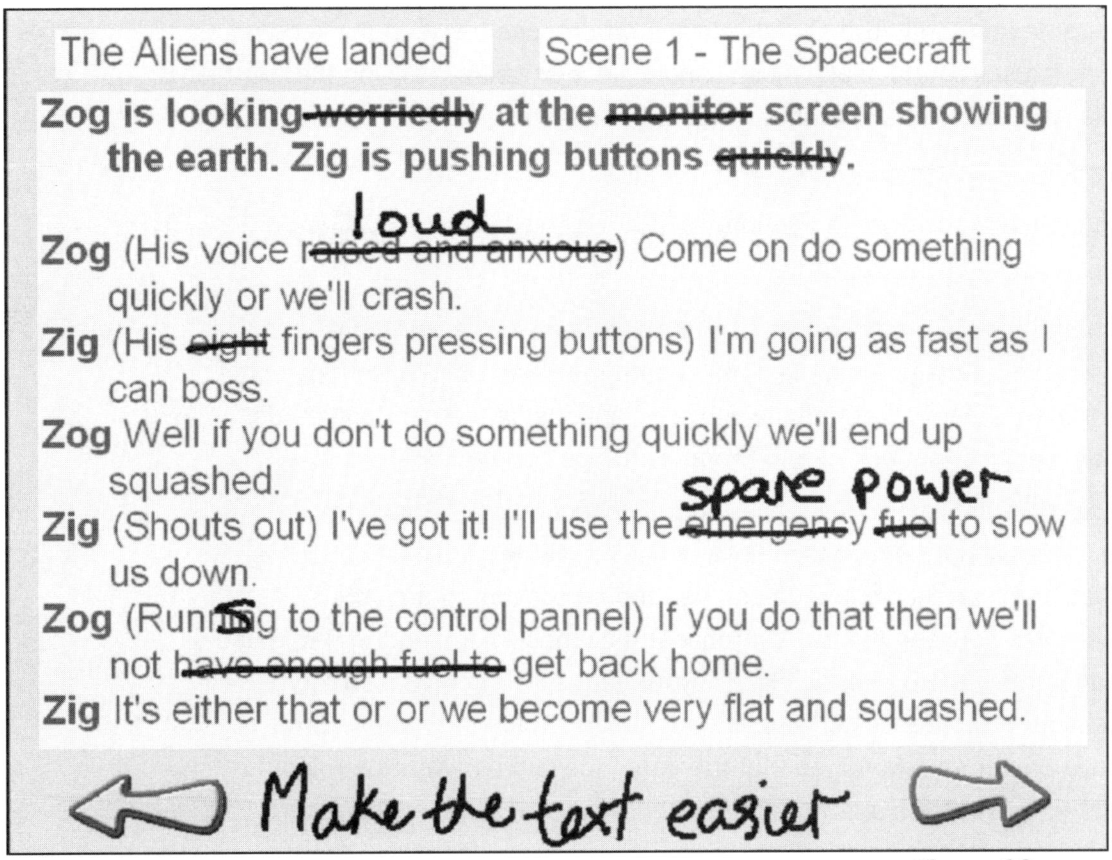

Figure 20

Sentence construction and punctuation

6 Display a text without commas or colons on the IWB and ask the children to insert the punctuation using the pen tool.

7 Display some text containing dialogue and ask the children to use the highlighter tool to mark text on various punctuation points to do with the dialogue, e.g. 66 and 99, place commas before the speech marks, dialogue in narrative is on separate lines.

8 Revise work on verbs, e.g. use the highlighter or pen tool to identify verbs in the text in the present tense, in the past tense, in the future tense, in the interrogative or imperative forms.

9 On the IWB, display some instructional text that contains imperatives. Get the children to come out and show, with the highlighter or pen tool, where the imperative verbs are.

Term 2 Sentence level work

Grammatical awareness

The work covered in numbers 1–4 has been dealt with in previous sections.

Sentence construction and punctuation

5 Display a piece of text without punctuation on the IWB and get the children to add in commas, colons, etc. using the pen tool.

6 Make notes on the IWB that highlight the differences between spoken and written language. You could show a short piece of text containing the points written below and then speak the passage as you might recount it.

- Writing should make sense away from its immediate context.
- Punctuation replaces intonation.
- Sentences are complete.

7 On the IWB, display a collection of signs and headlines taken from newspapers or magazines, e.g. 'Police shot man with knife', 'Nothing acts faster than Anadin', 'Baby changing room' and, using the pen tool, model any ambiguities that come from these sentence contractions.

8 On the IWB, display two sentences with a collection of conjunctions underneath and then model combining them together using a connective. The children can then come up and use the select tool to drag the connectives between the two sentences to connect them, and they can use the annotating (pen) tool to delete any full stops. They could also reorder sentences using the select tool, or use the edit function on the IWB to remove printed text words so that the sentence can be altered. (Using the on-screen keyboard might work here.) Add more words using character recognition or the annotating tool.

9 Identify clauses through the knowledge of commas in sentences, and display and identify subordinate clauses by inserting commas into a correct space. Note the role that the comma plays. You will have to model this on the IWB. Children could then use the highlighter tool to show subordinate clauses in displayed text.

10 Display a text on the IWB and get the children to highlight any pronouns. Then, with the pen tool, get them to link the pronouns to the noun to which they refer by drawing a connecting arrow.

Term 3 Sentence level work

Grammatical awareness

Numbers 1 and 2 have been covered in earlier sections.

3 Display text with prepositions in them. Get the children to highlight each preposition and see if they can substitute them with another one. Note what effect this has on meaning. This could be done using the rubber tool, the annotate tool or the pen tool.

Sentence construction and punctuation

4 Display a text without commas on the IWB and invite the children to insert the commas using the pen tool.

5 Revise the use of apostrophes for possession. Have some text with the apostrophes missing and get the children, using the pen tool, to insert them where there is possession.

6 Investigate clauses.

- Display text on the IWB and get the children to come out and highlight the main clause.
- Get the children to use a different colour and highlight other clauses.
- Demonstrate how clauses are connected together by combining three short sentences into one. Display three short sentences on the IWB and model how these can be made into one sentence with the use of commas. (Use the pen or select tool depending on whether you have created your writing in pen-tool mode or in text mode.)

7 Create text that needs to be made longer by adding connectives. Display the text on the IWB and ask the children to come out and identify where a connective can be added by annotating over that part of the sentence where they think a connective could go. Alternatively, have a list of connectives that can be dragged with a select tool to a correct place.

Term 1 Text level work

Fiction and Poetry

Reading comprehension

1 Analyse the features of a good opening, and compare a number of story openings by using the pen or highlighter tool. On the IWB, display various kinds of story openings. Ask the children to say what kind of story they are looking at the beginning of. On further flipchart/notebook pages, insert pictures as a stimulus to create ideas for a story opening and ask children to create their own at the IWB or away from the board. Do this for other story beginnings, like description, flashback, action and so on. Other groups of children could create word-processed story beginnings that can be loaded onto the computer controlling the IWB and displayed to the rest of the class. Alternatively, visit **www.sutton.lincs.sch.uk/pages/zone/story/start.html** to find work on story openings.

2 Over a period of time, explore two stories and, on the IWB, make notes on how they are built up, any sequences, any problems and their resolution. Work on one story first and then go on to the next story and do the same. From the notes you have made, compare similarities and differences. You, the teacher, can act as scribe. Saving and resaving flipchart or notebook files is a definite advantage here.

3 Investigate how character is presented. On the IWB, display texts that have dialogue relating to a character, action or description and how these relate to other characters. Ask the children to say what the piece of dialogue tells

them about the character, and then you can make notes on the IWB or use the highlighter tool to mark relevant texts.

4 Consider how texts can be rooted in the writer's experience, for example historical events and places, experiences of wartime, friendship or holidays. One approach would be to show a video on the IWB of a wartime experience and discuss how it might have affected a particular author who wrote about the war. You could then take notes on the IWB.

5 Display an extract from a play and get the children to highlight dialogue, stage directions, words and gestures. They could also highlight any places where tension can be built up.

6 On the IWB, display a selection of poems by the same poet and read them to the whole class. Begin to identify similarities about the style of the poems by highlighting similar rhyming patterns of words that recur in all the poems, or a recurring theme.

7 Analyse how a poem can be made up. For example, you could display a poem on the IWB and identify full rhymes and half rhymes by asking the children to come out and highlight them. You could also use the pen tool.

8 Display text that has examples of word play and ask the children to highlight any that they spot. Discuss what the children find.

9 Display a piece of text on the IWB and read it out. Ask the children to empathise with the characters and think what it would have been like if they were there. The children could come out to the IWB and write what it would be like if they were that particular character or if they were in that particular situation. Other groups would work away from the board using either paper or ICT to carry out the exercise and then load results onto the IWB computer for further discussion. The children could talk about what they have written in a plenary session.

10 Read a book or extracts from a book and evaluate it. Have a template in Word or on an IWB flipchart/notebook file and act as scribe, or a child could come out and write. Fill in the template with details of what people thought about the book. You could use something called 4Book Reviews from the 2Simple family of software, which gives you a pre-made template enabling you to use a keyboard or the pen tool to fill it out.

11 This links to number 1. You can explain different ways of starting your story. You could display a story that has the beginning missing and get the children to write in various openings that might fit the particular piece of text – it could be action or description, for example. It's probably best done as a group activity at a board.

12 Make up a PowerPoint presentation or flipchart/notebook file of a classic text, e.g. an extract from a Shakespeare play, and display it. Find pictures on the Internet to include. Then use the IWB to make notes, with you acting as scribe, on why the children continue to like this particular type of text or why they dislike it (see Figure 21).

Figure 21

Writing composition

13 Display the blurb from a book on the IWB. Get the children to make a prediction about whether they will like the book or what might happen in the story.

15 Use the IWB to introduce new characters into a story. You will need to read the story to the children then, on the IWB, display some pictures of characters that you might want them to put in. Away from the board, get the children to write a few sentences about a character, then invite them out to the front of the class to talk about this new character. They could use the IWB to write about it. If ICT skills are strong, they can type a description in Word, load it onto the display computer then display it to the rest of the class.

16 Display a poem on the IWB and ask the children to highlight words that show feelings or moods.

17 Display texts that contain several metaphors and ask the children to highlight them so they get the idea of what metaphors are. Then, on a new flipchart/notebook page, display some texts that need metaphors putting in and have a selection of words at the bottom that would fit as metaphors. Ask the children to use the select tool to drag them in to the right place, or you could write them in using the pen tool.

18 Ask a group of children to work at the IWB to create their own playscript. Have a template prepared for them and then they can interact with each other and use either the typewriting tool or the pen tool to write the playscript out.

19 Place a short extract from a playscript on the IWB and, as a group, get the children to annotate over it so that they can prepare for a performance. They can make notes on who is going to do and say what.

20 If you have the Promethean ActiveVote, you could evaluate any performance by the children using these devices. They are costly but allow instant feedback on any activity you do. You can name voters or keep them anonymous so that confidence is not dented. If your school is large enough (or well financed enough) then this system would add an extra dimension to your teaching from the point of view of assessment.

Non-fiction

Reading comprehension

21 Display a sports report or any other recounted text and ask the children to highlight where the introduction is, whether there is any sequencing, where any illustrations and connectives are, so that become familiar with the features of a recounted text.

22 Display a short instructional text on the IWB and read through it as a whole class. Interrogate the children to elicit:

- what the purpose of the text is
- how is it organised
- how clear it is.

Ask the children to come out and annotate on the IWB, highlighting these points.

Writing composition

24 Display examples of recounts that you might give to a close friend or, in contrast, to an unknown reader. Encourage the children to use this to help them work away from the IWB to create their own recount based on a subject or personal experience. If they create their work as a word-processed document they can then display it on the IWB for whole-class discussion.

25 Get the children to write out some instructional texts on word processors and save their work to disk. Load it onto the machine that runs the IWB, display the text and analyse it. See if you can get the class to follow the instructions they have written. A topic could be 'rules for a game'.

26 Demonstrate on the IWB the making of notes for different purposes, e.g. display a text and highlight key words, list cues for a talk.

27 Use the IWB to create a list of abbreviations that children could use in note-taking. Display a list of commonly recurring words on a flipchart and

ask the children to come out and write down a symbol, e.g. the plus symbol for 'and'. Do this task for all the words you have written down.

Term 2 Text level work

Fiction and Poetry

Reading comprehension

1 Identify and classify the features of myths, legends and fables. Read the children a classical myth, legend or fable, display a shortened version of it on the IWB and get them to work out what the typical features of the genre are. For example, in a fairy tale there would be some sort of magic going on, perhaps a magic mirror. The children would highlight where this is mentioned in the text. You might need to shorten the text slightly in order to include all the different features.

2 Investigate different versions of the same story. Create two different versions of a story on the IWB and display them. You could then annotate the similarities of the differences between the two texts.

3 Display a short text on an IWB and then give an oral version of it to the class. Model similarities and differences the children may find.

4 Display texts of a narrative poem on the IWB and read it as whole-class activity. Annotate and highlight as appropriate.

5 Again, reading the text from the IWB, perform a poem in a variety of ways. Half the class can do one verse, the other half the other verse, or certain groups can do the main part of the poem and others do the chorus, and so on.

6 Display various kinds of poems on the IWB (this could be done through the Internet, for example). Get the children to identify what kinds of poems they are, e.g. a ballad, a rap or a narrative poem, and annotate typical features.

7 Use the IWB to compile an anthology of favourite poems that you can revisit and add to. Save the flipchart(s) that you have created.

8 Display a piece of text on the IWB. Is it the author saying something, or is it a narrator or a villain saying something? What's the perspective? Ask the children to highlight words that give away who is saying what and from what point of view the story is being written.

9 Create a flipchart/notebook file showing different genres of fiction. Ask the children to highlight literal language and figurative language.

10 Display text showing examples of literal and figurative language on the IWB and use the pen or highlighter tool to outline differences.

Writing composition

11 This would be group work at the IWB. The children could get together and construct their own learning by writing a version of a myth, a legend or a fable they have already come across. It may be useful to use the IWB to make notes and then go away and do it later on. Other groups could create word-processed work and display their versions on the computer controlling the IWB for whole-class discussion and evaluation.

12 Display a poem on the IWB and ask the children to come out and create an additional verse for it. This can be done in groups away from the board, with one group working at the IWB. Other groups could create word-processed work and display their versions on the computer controlling the IWB for whole-class discussion and evaluation.

13 On the IWB, display work that children have created, and annotate it with them so it can be produced in a final form. (The work would have to be word processed or scanned.) This would be group work, or perhaps a class story.

Non-fiction

Reading comprehension

14 On the IWB, make notes of the story outline from a story that you have been reading. Groups of children can then recount the story orally.

15 Display an explanatory text on the IWB and act as scribe to highlight structures of the text. Highlight any passive language, technical vocabulary, hypothetical language, complex sentences and use the work that you have done to get the children to create their own explanatory text. This can be done in groups away from the board, with one group working on the IWB. Other groups could create word-processed work and display their versions on the computer controlling the IWB for whole-class discussion and evaluation.

17 Create a flipchart on the IWB showing a contents page and an index page. Use it to show children how to locate information confidently and efficiently.

An encyclopaedia CD-ROM (e.g. *The Oxford Children's Encyclopaedia*) could be controlled and annotated over for the same purpose.

19 Display different evaluations of a written text on the IWB and make comparisons. Use the pen or highlighter tool.

Writing composition

21 As an exercise, ask the children to write up notes they have made on a given topic. These will need to be word processed so they can be displayed on the IWB and then discussed by looking at style, vocabulary and presentation.

22 Using the same method as in number 21, ask the children to write short non-chronological reports or explanatory texts and show them to the rest of the class. In doing so, number 24 will be covered as children will be evaluating their own and others' work.

23 Show all work on the IWB with acknowledgements to external sources.

24 Use the IWB to display work for evaluation.

Term 3 Text level work

Fiction and Poetry

Reading comprehension

1 Display texts from different cultures and use the pen or highlighter tool to identify relevant features and, if possible, get the children to relate them to their own experiences.

2 Display a text on the IWB and highlight parts of it to show points of view.

3 When working on number 2, discuss how you can change the point of view. You can act as scribe.

4 Read a poem displayed on the IWB for performance practise.

5 Compile a class anthology that is displayed on the IWB and use it to ask children why they chose particular pieces.

6 Display text related to older literature on the IWB and read it out to the class. Look at TV highlights of classics (e.g. *Pride and Prejudice*). Highlight or annotate any differences in language.

Writing composition

7 Display a text that is written from a point of view of a character and ask the children to retell that incident from another character's point of view. This can be done in groups away from the board, with one group working on the IWB. Other groups could create word-processed work and display their versions on the computer controlling the IWB for whole-class discussion and evaluation.

9 Write some text in the style of an author. This can be done in groups away from the board but a group could work the IWB, too. Other groups could create word-processed work and display their versions on the computer controlling the IWB for whole-class discussion and evaluation.

10 Write about a novel or story. This can be done in groups away from the board, with one group working on the IWB. Other groups could create word-processed work and display their versions on the computer controlling the IWB for whole-class discussion and evaluation.

11 Using performance poems as a model (displayed on the IWB), children write out their own poems. This can be done in groups away from the board, with one group working on the IWB. Other groups could create word-processed work and display their versions on the computer controlling the IWB for whole-class discussion and evaluation.

Non-fiction

Reading comprehension

12 Display letters taken from newspapers or magazines on the IWB (they can be typed or scanned). Read and evaluate them, annotating or highlighting where appropriate for evidence of protest, complaint or persuasion.

13 Read other scanned newspaper extracts on the IWB and annotate for any bias, half truths or ambiguity. Is there any opinion disguised as fact?

14 Develop a collection of texts for display on the IWB that show persuasion or clarity. Annotate over them as required.

15 Collect a series of persuasive devices and phrases on the IWB that can be used for written work.

16 Display a text on the IWB and highlight extracts that are key to the meaning of the passage, thus abbreviating it.

Writing composition

17 Write a draft letter for a real purpose, e.g. putting forward a point of view. This can be done in groups away from the board, with one group working on the IWB. Other groups could create word-processed work and display their versions on the computer controlling the IWB for whole-class discussion and evaluation.

18 Write a commentary on a given issue. This can be done in groups away from the board, with one group working on the IWB. Other groups could create word-processed work and display their versions on the computer controlling the IWB for whole-class discussion and evaluation.

19 Ask the children to construct an argument to deliver to the rest of the class. One group could use a template you have made on the IWB. Other groups could create word-processed work and display their versions on the computer controlling the IWB for whole-class discussion and evaluation.

Year 6

Term 1 Word level work

Much of the work here is revision from previous years, especially Year 5, and ideas for use of the IWB would be repeated, so I have only elaborated on objectives that I feel need reinforcing.

Spelling strategies

Numbers 1, 2 and 3 have been covered in Year 5.

Spelling conventions and rules

4 Please see Year 5 Word work, Term 3, number 4.

5 Create a flipchart of word roots and ask the children to add prefixes and suffixes to them with the pen tool. They could also drag selected parts of words together to create new ones. These are for the following prefixes and suffixes: aero, aqua, audi, bi, cede, clude, con, cred, duo, log(o)(y), hyd(ro)(ra), in, micro, oct, photo, port, prim, scribe, scope, sub, tele, tri, ex.

6 Display the following connectives on the IWB: therefore, notwithstanding, furthermore. (You can add more.) Type out their meanings, but jumble them up. Ask the children to use the select tool to match the words to the correct meanings.

Vocabulary extension

7 In a random order, display words on the IWB that have fallen out of use (e.g. yonder, thither) and their modern counterparts. Use the select tool to match them up.

8 Model how to find the origins of proper names by searching for clues on the Internet. Annotate results as appropriate.

9 Create a flipchart collection of new words that have been added to the English language, e.g. trainers, wheelie.

10 Scan a page from an etymological dictionary (a dictionary that shows the origins of words) and highlight and annotate as necessary. You might like to use a document camera here if you have one.

Term 2 Word level work

Spelling strategies

Numbers 1, 2 and 3 have been covered in Year 5.

Spelling conventions and rules

Numbers 4 and 5 ask the teacher to revise and consolidate work related to spelling. The objectives here have been covered in earlier sections, so I suggest you review your own school's source material, e.g. Letts Literacy books, and convert the content into flipchart/notebook file format. This would be an advanced skill, but is a rich source of content material to fit onto your IWBs.

Vocabulary extension

6 Display a collection of proverbs on the IWB and ask the children to give meanings orally or in writing. New ones should be added as they are discovered. Proverbs and explanations could be displayed in a mixed-up format and then matched up using the select tool.

Term 3 Word level work

Spelling strategies

Numbers 1, 2 and 3 have been covered in Year 5.

Spelling conventions and rules

Number 4 asks the teacher to revise and consolidate work related to spelling. The objectives here have been covered in earlier sections, so I suggest you review your own school's source material, e.g. Letts Literacy books, and convert the content into flipchart format. This would be an advanced skill, but is a rich source of content material to fit onto your IWBs.

Vocabulary extension

5 Invent words on the IWB using known roots, prefixes and suffixes. Use the select tool to join words like *vacca* to *phobe* to create the word *vaccaphobe* (someone who has a fear of cows). You'll need to create your own list for the children to join together

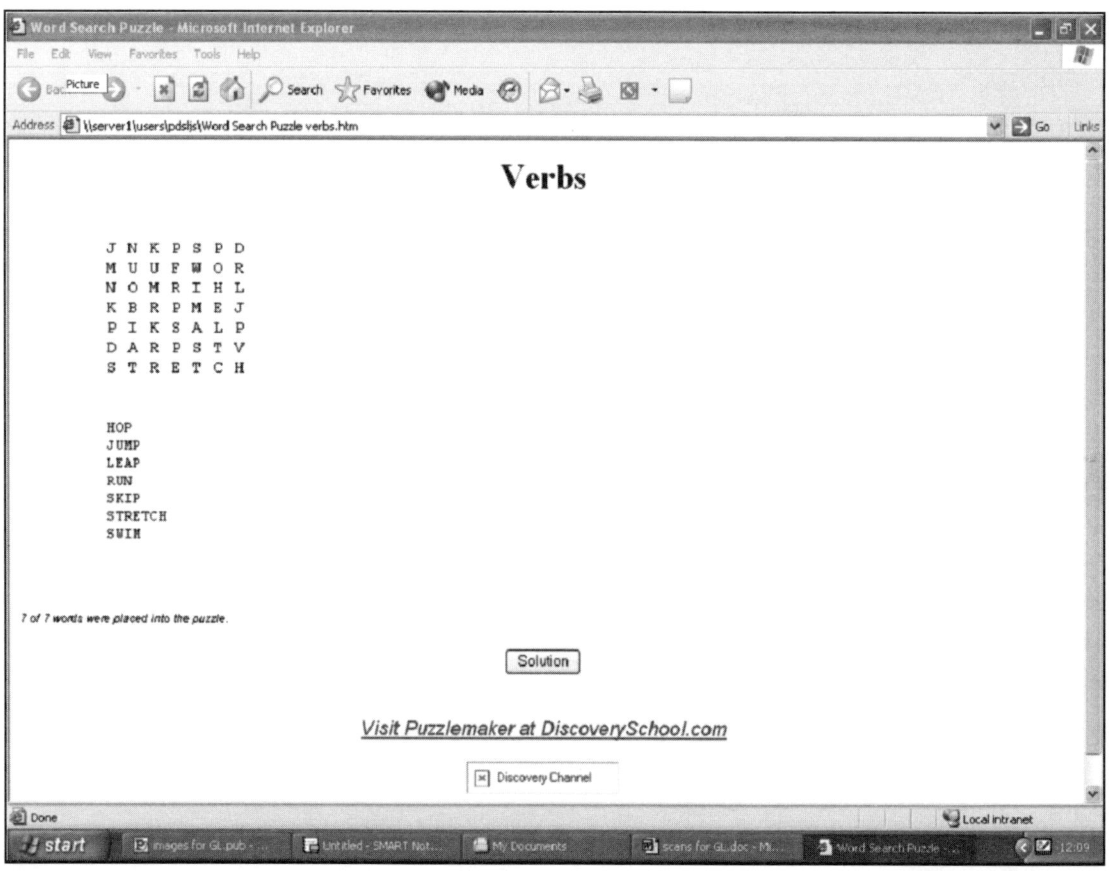

Figure 22

6 Display a wordseach you have created on the IWB and then highlight relevant words (see Figure 22). You could use **www.puzzlemaker.com** to create your wordsearches. (You can create more than wordsearches on this website.)

7 Be the scribe for children creating new words, similes and metaphors. Save these words on your IWB software.

Term 1 Sentence level work

Grammatical awareness

Numbers 1 to 3 in this section are revision topics that have been already been covered. Please look back at Years 4 and 5 for ideas relating to these numbers.

Sentence construction and punctuation

4 Investigate connecting words and phrases.

- Create a collection of such words and save them on an IWB flipchart/notebook file.
- Highlight texts displayed on the IWB for ways of connectivity. Use the pen or highlighter tool.
- Classify connectives related to different kinds of text, e.g. by position (besides, nearby, by), by sequence (firstly, secondly), by logic (therefore, so, consequently). Insert these connectives into a cloze text using the select tool.
- Identify connectives that have multiple purposes (on, under, besides). Create exercises that allow you to insert these connectives into text displayed on an IWB.

5 Form complex sentences on the IWB, then use the pen tool to annotate over or in between text that is missing connectives. Highlight the different clauses in a sentence with different colours.

6 With the pen tool, punctuate a text that is missing colons, commas, dashes and brackets.

Term 2 Sentence level work

Grammatical awareness

1 On the IWB, display a text that contains active and passive verbs and annotate or highlight them using appropriate tools. Change text from the active to the passive and vice versa by adding extra vocabulary, etc. using the pen tool.

2 Understand the features of formal official language.

- On the IWB, display examples that have been collected over a period of time and annotate as appropriate.

- Highlight text displayed on the IWB using these language conventions: the impersonal voice, the imperative voice, formal vocabulary.

Sentence construction and punctuation

3 Revise work on complex sentences. This has been covered in earlier sections, but a mainstay idea would be to display, on the IWB, a text that can be annotated over to show main and subordinate clauses, connectives and punctuation. (This could be done by having these elements missing in the text and then inserted using the pen tool.)

4 Contract sentences by highlighting key words and phrases using the pen or highlighter tool. Get the children to work in groups (one at the board) to rewrite a shortened version of the original.

5 Conditional sentences.

- Display some text on the IWB and use the pen or highlighter tool to show words indicating the conditional, e.g. if ..., then, might, could, would.
- Ask children to create their own conditional sentences. This can be done in groups away from the board, with one group working at the IWB. Other groups could create word-processed work and display their versions on the computer controlling the IWB for whole-class discussion and evaluation.

Term 3 Sentence level work

Grammatical awareness

1 This section is revision of the use of:

- stories and novels
- recounts
- instructional texts
- reports
- explanatory texts
- persuasive texts discursive texts.

For all these you can follow the pattern of displaying the relevant text on the IWB, and annotating or using the pen tool accordingly. Other details have already been covered. especially in Years 4 and 5.

Sentence construction and punctuation

3 The use of formal writing in terms of the impersonal and passive voice and the management of complex sentences has been thoroughly reviewed in previous sections.

4 Create clauses on the IWB that are separate units of text and then manipulate them using the select tool to achieve different effects.

Term 1 Text level work

Fiction and Poetry

Reading comprehension

1 Compare and evaluate a novel or play with a TV version. Ask the children to read extracts of the novel or the play, then show the TV version on the IWB. Start to compare the plot and the characters and the differences between the two forms (e.g. you don't see the setting in the book but you see it on the TV, and the narrator is lost in the TV version). If you are interested in creating your own stories and filming them, then this may be the ideal objective for you to refer to.

2 Have an extract of a novel displayed on the IWB and make sure you can identify the narrator (use annotation or highlighting). Ask the children if this point of view influences the reader's view of what happened and explain how the events might look from a different point of view. Create a second flipchart/notebook page that shows the point of view of a different character in the same story. Highlight relevant text. On a final flipchart page, get a group of children to brainstorm and create their own point of view of the novel or text that they have read.

3 Read a book, a story or an extract with the children and get them to articulate their responses. Your children should be able to act as scribes by now. On the IWB they compare the effect that the text has on different readers.

4 Create a flipchart or page on the IWB that tells the children something about established authors and their styles. Highlight or annotate appropriately and ask the children to explain preferences.

5 Act as scribe and take notes on the IWB about how an author writes his or her books, what kind of books he or she has done and what the children think. Save the work to return to it at a later date.

Writing composition

6 Create text on a particular book or story on an IWB flipchart/notebook file. On a second flipchart/notebook page, create a similar piece of text in the style of the first and encourage the children to use this as a reference to create their own version. Word-processed work can be loaded onto the computer controlling the IWB, so all work can be reviewed and assessed.

7 On the IWB, scribe the plan for the plot, characterisation and structure of some narrative writing. This can be a whole-class activity. Afterwards, children can come up in groups to work at the board while the rest of the class works on paper or on computers to display work at a later date.

8 Display some text on the IWB, then summarise it by highlighting keywords. Invite the children to come up and, on a new flipchart page, write out the shortened version. This could be done as whole-class activity or as a group

activity. The children could then be given a text to summarise on their own in a given number of words.

9 Display an extract from a story on a flipchart and then, with the children, transfer this into a playscript format. The children could then come up in groups and do their own formats on the IWB.

10 A group of children could write a poem on the IWB, concentrating on personification, and then present it to the class. Word-processed work can be loaded onto the computer controlling the IWB, so all work can be reviewed and assessed.

Non-fiction

Reading comprehension

11 Distinguish between biography and autobiography.

- Put the words 'biography' and 'autobiography', and their meanings, on the IWB. Ask the children to use the select tool to match up the each word to its correct meaning.
- Show text that is fact, opinion or fiction, relating to a person, and highlight or use the pen tool appropriately.

12 On a flipchart, display various non-fiction texts such as such as reviews, periodicals, reports and leaflets, and annotate appropriately (see Figure 23).

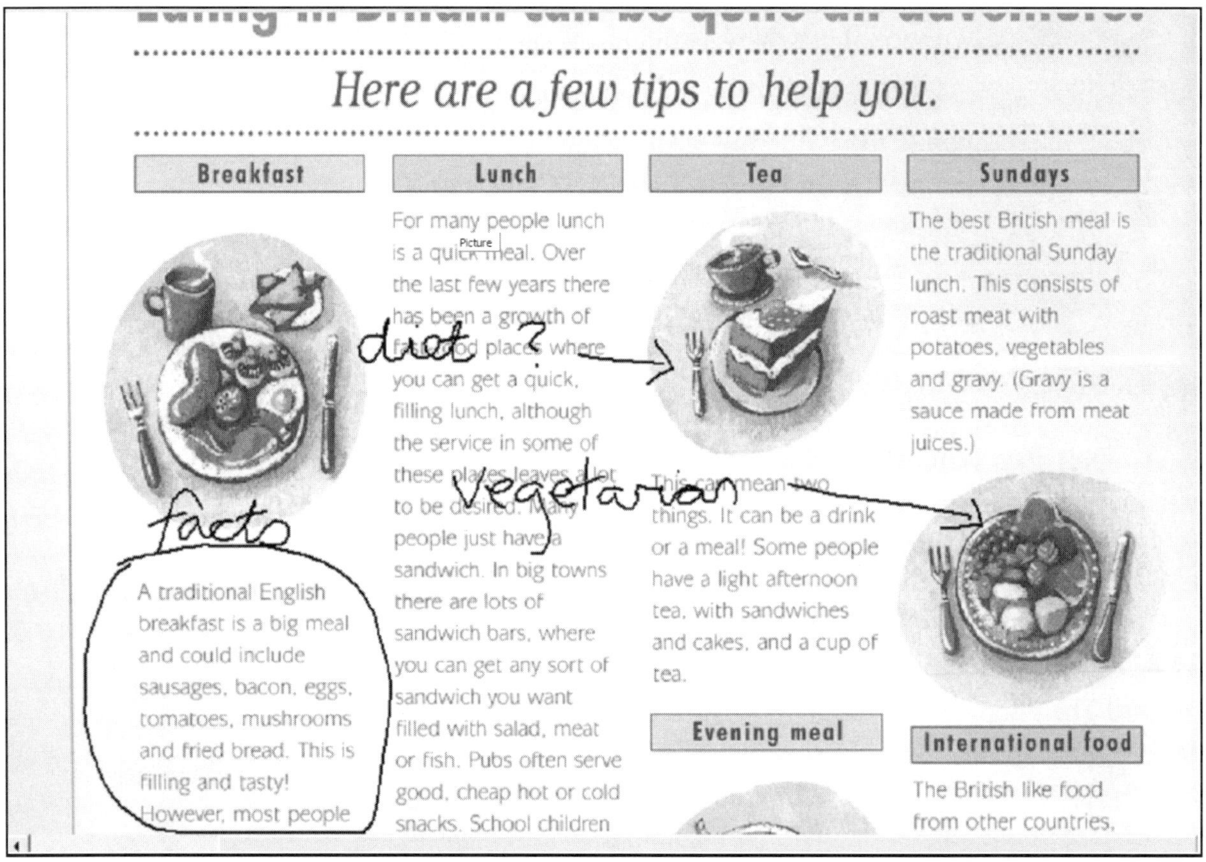

Figure 23

13 Explain the features of non-chronological reports. Display a non-chronological report on the board and get the children to:

- highlight any generalisations
- highlight any descriptive language
- highlight any impersonal language
- annotate the present tense.

Writing composition

14 Practise skills of biographical and autobiographical writing.

- On a flipchart, display a CV. With the children, go over how to create one by annotating or highlighting. Ask the children, in groups, to create a CV of their own. One group could work at the IWB. Word-processed work can be loaded onto the computer controlling the IWB, so all work can be reviewed and assessed. You may like to use a capture tool for this activity (usually the tool looks like a camera).
- On a flipchart, display a biographical account based on an Internet search. Highlight various parts of the text.
- Describe a person from a particular perspective, e.g. how they might be seen by the police. Make notes on the IWB.
- Show text on the IWB that might have come from a school report or a newspaper obituary.

15 Groups of children could do some writing in a journalistic style for review on the IWB. Word-processed work can be loaded onto the computer controlling the IWB, so all work can be reviewed and assessed. (Journalistic style relates to balanced reporting, catering for public interest, reader interest and selection and presentation of information.)

16 Create a report on a real event and display results on the IWB for discussion and annotation.

17 Write as in number 16, but a non-chronological report linked to another subject.

18 Show the children how to work on Microsoft Publisher via the IWB, so that they can compile a newspaper page. This would involve capturing icons, highlighting and using the pen tool.

Term 2 Text level work

Fiction and Poetry

Reading comprehension

1 Use the IWB to understand aspects of narrative structure.

- By annotating or highlighting text displayed on the IWB, explain how chapters or paragraphs link together.

- Show how time is portrayed using a flowchart, flashback, stories within stories, dreams, and how the passing of time is conveyed to the reader using words. Ask the children to highlight them on the flipchart.

2 Analyse how a paragraph is written. Have a paragraph displayed on a flipchart and get the children to highlight the main idea of that paragraph.

3 Display a poem on a flipchart and get the children to annotate rhyme patterns and figurative language, and to find multiple layers of meaning.

4 Display some humorous verse on a flipchart. Ask the children to use the pen tool to underline wordplay or nonsense words, or where the appeal of the poem lies in the phrases or words.

5 Display a poem on a flipchart and, using the highlighter or pen tool, analyse how any messages, moods or feelings and attitudes are conveyed in poetry.

6 Display a poem on a flipchart and read it with the class. Ask them to come out and, using the highlighter tool, find any meanings that are implied or multi-layered.

7 Display a literary effect on a flipchart and highlight key features, e.g. plot structure.

8 Study a text displayed on a flipchart. Highlight language that evokes a particular response, e.g. for suspense, highlight the words that build up that suspense.

9 Revisit poems from significant poets from the past by displaying them through the Internet on a flipchart. Alternatively, you could type them out or make use of a document camera.

Writing composition

10 Create text of different genres and display them on a flipchart. Challenge the children to brainstorm different endings for the texts. As a group, on a new flipchart page, ask the children to create an alternative ending to a text, or add to the text and display it to the class. Word-processed work can be loaded into the computer controlling the IWB, so all work can be reviewed and assessed.

11 Ask a group of children to come to the IWB to brainstorm how to use flashback in a story to convey the passing of time (see Figure 24). Give an example on a flipchart page, showing a picture to help, and using some text which has been linked to a sound file. (Use Promethean software or Granada Writer/Textease.)

12 As part of studying a particular genre, e.g. science-fiction or horror stories, get the children to create an extended piece of writing on a flipchart. The children work in groups, each group writing a different part of the story, page by page, to build up an anthology.

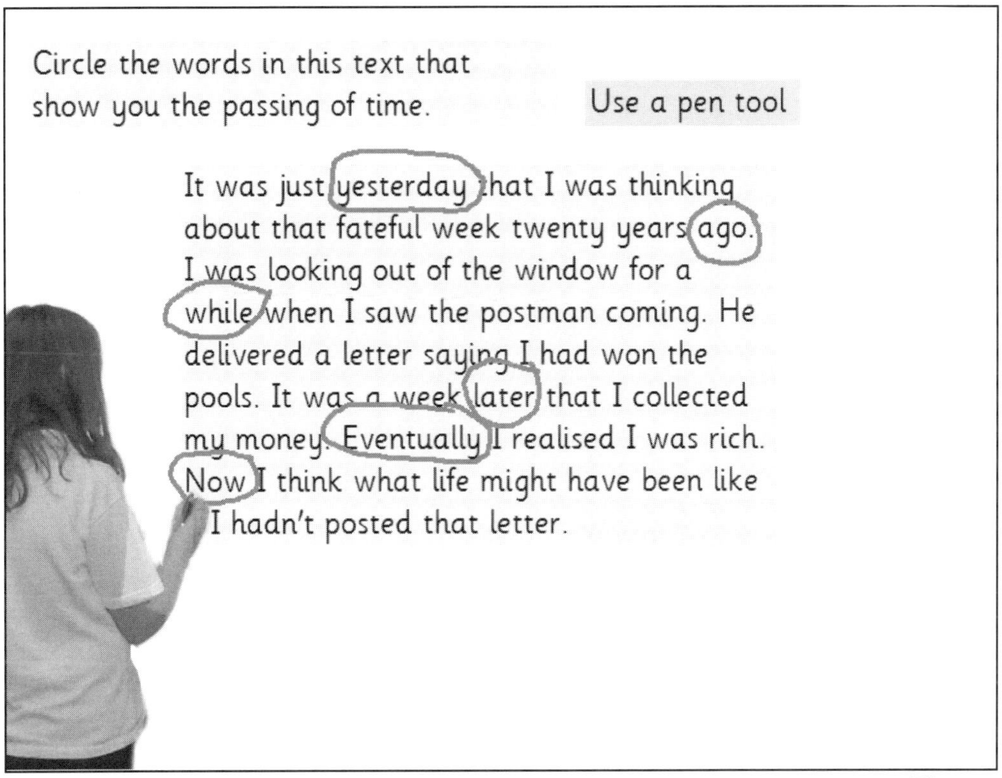

Figure 24

13 Create a parody of a literary text by describing characters, plot structure and language. Initially you can act as scribe, writing on the IWB. A group of children can then come up and, on a new flipchart page, create the text parody.

14 Write a commentary or summary of text and display it on the IWB. In groups, the children write their commentaries on the board. Word-processed work can be loaded onto the computer controlling the IWB, so all work can be reviewed and assessed. Use the style 'The writer says that ....'

Non-fiction

Reading comprehension

15 Discuss how arguments are constructed. Display a text relating to an argument on the IWB and get the children to highlight:

- any persuasive examples
- any texts that pre-empt or answer a potential objection
- text that appeals to the known views of the audience.

16 Use a writing frame to identify the features of a written argument.

- Summarise different sides of an argument on the IWB.
- Highlight the strengths and weaknesses of different positions.
- Give a personal opinion clearly. A group of children could come out to the IWB and create the argument by working collaboratively together.

17 Display legal documents, consumer information, layouts and instructions on the IWB. Analyse official language by highlighting. A document camera might come in handy here or, failing that, use a scanner.

Writing composition

18 Show the children how to construct an effective argument by displaying a template on the IWB that:

- develops the point logically
- persuades
- anticipates any objections
- takes account of known views.

19 Display text of a controversial issue on the IWB and ask the children to summarise the views orally. They should analyse the strengths and weaknesses of the various arguments. They then work in groups to create a balanced report. One group could work on the IWB while other groups create word-processed work. These versions could later be loaded onto the computer controlling the IWB for whole-class discussion and evaluation. Remember to annotate and highlight appropriately.

20 On the IWB, display different modes of standard English, e.g. legal language and questionnaires, and analyse them using the annotation or highlighter tool.

Term 3 Text level work

Fiction and Poetry

Reading comprehension

1 On the IWB, display an abridged piece of writing by a particular author and highlight aspects to illustrate the author's style.

2 Display a series of linked poems on a flipchart/notebook page and, using the highlighter or pen tool, identify how they relate to each other, e.g. cycles of poems about the seasons.

3 Display a poem on the IWB and get the children to highlight various aspects of style.

4 Display a poem on the IWB and ask the children how it has impacted on them. Annotate or highlight accordingly.

5 Display two or three extracts of a writer's work on the IWB and look at various aspects of the style. Compare them after annotation and discussion.

6 Display two or three extracts of different writers' work and compare them after annotation and discussion.

Writing composition

7 Annotate a passage displayed on the IWB in response to specific questions.

9 On the IWB, create a summary of a book or part of a book via annotation and discussion. Ask a group of children to come out to the IWB to collectively create their own summary.

10 On the IWB, show an example of a synopsis for the back cover of a book. Get the children to create their own synopsis, working at the IWB or in groups on computers, or writing freehand.

11 Ask a group of children to write a review for a specific audience on the IWB.

12 Display a text on the IWB and use the pen or highlighter tool to show styles, strengths or weaknesses, different values.

13 Over a period of time, ask groups of children to create poems of a similar theme and display and present their results to their peers on the IWB.

14 As in number 13, but instead of a poem, ask the children to create an extended story.

Non-fiction

Reading comprehension

15 Highlight and annotate features of an explanatory text on the IWB.

16 Display a text on the IWB and use the highlighter or pen tool to show the features of impersonal formal language in the shape of the present tense and the passive voice.

17 & 18 As a class activity, ask the class to appraise quickly a text displayed on the IWB, annotating and highlighting accordingly.

19 Display a range of non-fiction texts and annotate appropriately.

Writing composition

20 Highlight text displayed on the IWB for use of present tense and passive voice to indicate impersonal writing.

21 Display text on the IWB that has no paragraphing, and work with the children to show where paragraphing could take place. Annotate or highlight appropriately.

Sources and further information

So, now that we have all these ideas, where do we get the source materials to convert them into reality? As a teacher, my first port of call would be to look at all the literacy materials at my disposal and convert the exercises into flipchart or notebook activities. I would only do two or three pages, as each page can involve five minutes' work. Don't be too fancy and waste time on creating masterpieces of multimedia – create work simply and without fuss. If you are spending hours on flipcharts or notebooks then you are wasting valuable free time that could be spent having a life! Yes, you must prepare work and this new field will take a little learning, but keep everything in proportion. Do a little at first, then, as you speed up, you'll produce more. The Letts literacy materials are a good starting point for this, but you can use whichever scheme your school has.

If you work in Year 6 there is a lot of revision and consolidation to be done, so I would look at resources in book form and on the Internet, and then capture them into a flipchart or notebook file. Text can then be annotated over, highlighted or moved around. You can also begin to link text to images, sound and video. The drawback is, of course, time, so you will need to manage this sensibly so that you also have a life out of school.

The next port of call is to look at supportive software. This is crucial because in using third-party software that is whiteboard friendly, you will save precious time!

Software to support the use of an IWB in literacy lessons

When you get an IWB, there will probably be groans of 'Oh no, not more work!'. Relax! You can simply use what is already on the market to support your literacy lessons. It is sensible to use what is currently on the market as it will save you time – you won't have to learn how to run all the software on an IWB before you can quickly get started using one.

I haven't linked the software to specific ideas, as the descriptions I have provided below give you a comprehensive overall pattern of what you can use. You simply need to get hold of this software, review it and link it to the targets as defined in each year group. Then run the CD-ROM.

Reception and Key Stage 1 materials

- Granada Writer and Textease (Studio) are ideal word processors for this age range and IWB use as you can move text around the screen without restriction, and you can also draw next to text. It offers good versatility in the key mode of selecting and dragging, which is the most important interactive feature when using an IWB. Granada Writer/Textease (Studio) will work on any board, and with their built-in interactivity, one or the other is a <u>must</u> for IWB users. Easiteach Literacy, a development from Textease, is also well worth a look.

- 2Simple software is ideal for use from Early Years to Year 2, as you can progress from drawing simple pictures and writing captions to writing addresses on letters (very easily). The displays look good on a whiteboard, but the text, once written, does not move around as in Granada Writer/Textease (Studio), so you would need to use an on-screen keyboard to write with.
- You could easily use PowerPoint to create displays and talking books that would stimulate the children, but the slide shows are linear and text can't be moved around in an ad hoc manner. There is, however, a pen tool that allows you to write on screen, but this does not compare with the pen tools found on an IWB. You would also need to spend some time becoming a good PowerPoint user to create appealing displays. Textease has recently brought out a version similar to PowerPoint designed for children to use.
- There are many versions of word processors which will display text that can be annotated over using a pen tool. The most common of these are Talking First Word from RM, Writer from Blackcat and, of course, Word itself.
- Clicker4 is an innovative piece of software in that you have two screens to work on. The first is a grid of text, pictures or both. You click on a word and it is displayed on a writing screen. Words and sentences are also spoken. This piece of software lends itself to use on an IWB as Cricksoft (the software designers) have created hundreds of grids to cover activities in literacy lessons. They range from letter recognition, nursery rhymes and phonic work to talking books. This particular piece of software, I think, is a <u>must</u> for any school as it is not only excellent for literacy and SEN use, but will support all subjects across the curriculum. There's a resource for just about everything produced to run through Clicker4.

  They have downloads from their website for free, plus a whole range of CD-ROMs. Here are some useful titles:

  - *Clicker4* is your mainstay programme.
  - *Clicker animations* adds movement to your grids (very useful for IWB display).
  - *Clicker sounds* is useful for adding extra sounds to grids you have created.
  - They have CD-ROMs of resources ranging across the curriculum but with many literacy activities.
  - They have talking books in a range called *Planet Wobble* that contain literacy activities.
  - There is a range of non-fiction material differentiated for all levels. Titles range from *The Solar System* to *Minibeasts.*
  - There is a picture dictionary.
  - There is a CD-ROM on nursery rhymes.

These titles would work well on a large screen and would be interactive due to links to speech, animation and video.

- Sherston produces a whole range of CD-ROMs that seem ideal for use on an IWB and support literacy lessons. The following titles could be used at KS1:
  - *Sound Stories* – This CD-ROM can be displayed on an IWB to aid sound identification, recognise initial letters, develop alphabetical awareness and aid reading and spelling. There are 30 sound books covering letter sounds and rhymes suitable for work in Reception and Year 1.
  - *The Big ABC* – This CD-ROM can be displayed on an IWB to listen to rhymes for each letter of the alphabet, identify letters and read and spell words. It can be used for work in Reception and Year 1.
  - *Sound Activities* – This CD-ROM can be used on an IWB to display work in an interactive way on the identification of sounds, recognition of letters and the reading and spelling of words. It can be used for work in for work in Reception and Year 1
  - Oxford Reading Tree software, Stage 1 – This is the first in the series and, when displayed on an IWB, can be read by the whole class and annotated appropriately. This CD-ROM has sections of it that only speak, so it is suitable for Reception work.
  - Oxford Reading Tree software, Stages 2 and 3 – This is a collection of talking books for Reception and Year 1 and is suitable text level work for projection and annotation on an IWB.
  - Oxford Reading Tree software, Stages 4 and 5 – This is a further collection of stories stretching into Year 2. They could be used for whole-class teaching or for group work using an IWB.
  - Rhyme and Analogy Activity software Volume A – This is an interactive CD-ROM with listening, reading and rhyming activities enhancing phonological skills. The displays are ideal for projection on an IWB screen. This could be used for all of KS1.
  - Rhyme and Analogy Activity software Volume B – This is an interactive CD-ROM with activities based on aural and visual discrimination. It contains 24 rhyming families. It would be suitable for Year 2 and Year 3 work.
  - Literacy Box R, 1 and 2 – This is a collection of three CD-ROMs to cover word level work. Year R covers work in rhyme, identifying final and initial phonemes, letter sound association and alphabetic and phonic knowledge. Year 1 covers work on blending phonemes, identifying initial consonant clusters and spelling long vowel words. Year 2 covers work on long vowel phonemes, identifying syllables and spelling compound words.
  - Oxford Reading Tree Clipart (KS1) and Sherston's Curriculum Clipart (KS2) – These contain images that are great for the creation of resources to add to those you can buy in the form of a CD-ROM.

- *Nursery Rhyme Time* – This is a CD-ROM that contains 11 animated nursery rhymes that can be read, listened to or sung along with. This is suitable for KS1.
- *Teacher's Cupboard* – This is an adventure CD-ROM based on literacy activities, e.g. there's an 'I spy' game that involves spotting objects that begin with a specific initial letter sound.
- *Naughty Stories* – This is a CD-ROM containing 12 talking books.
- *Talking Topics* – This is a non-fiction talking CD-ROM based on the topics of pets, the body, homes, transport, the seashore and dinosaurs. This is a <u>must</u> for IWB use in KS1 to foster research and retrieval skills.

These titles all display well and are suitable for KS1. They are interactive and will save you time, in that once you have identified your activity and matched it to the NPS, you have an immediate resource to display and annotate on an IWB.

- Granada Learning has a good range of resources for IWB use in literacy lesson at KS1.
  - There is a set of three CD-ROMs called *Leaps and Bounds* that contain numerous literacy activities that will display well on an IWB.
  - Next comes a range of three CD-ROMs called *At the Doctor's, At the Vet's* and *At the Café*. They are creative and motivating CD-ROMs that can act as stating points for role-play activity.
  - *Fetch the Vet* is and interactive CD-ROM that contains video clips and early literacy activities that will display well on an IWB.
  - There is a set of phonics CD-ROMs called *Soundstart* (red and orange for Reception and Yellow for KS1). These are based around phonics activities taken from interactive on-screen stories.
  - If you are a fan of the Fuzzbuzz series, they are available and display well on an IWB (the material extends into KS2).
  - There is a series of CD-ROMs called Primary Literacy 1, 2 and 3 that contain interactive literacy ideas that would display well on an IWB.
  - *Ready for Writing* is a neat package to encourage creative writing, with a screen large enough to show well on an IWB and word lists that include audio. It would work well to model writing with a whole class and then in individual work, which can be saved and displayed on an IWB in a plenary session.
  - *My World 3* is a <u>must</u> for any IWB in that objects can be selected and moved across the screen independently, so that they can be very quickly used on an IWB without needing to spend too long learning how to use whiteboard software. You will first need to purchase *My World 3* and then there are the following titles available at £39.00 for a site licence:
  - *Literacy – The Early Years* – Here you get 19 discrete sets of screens ranging from alphabetical work to sounds and spelling. This CD-ROM is a <u>must</u> for all IWB users at KS1.

- *My World of Pictures and Words* – This CD-ROM relates to story telling for the early years, with screens available on *The Three Pigs*, *Fairy Tales* and *Phonics*. This CD-ROM is a must for all IWB users at KS1.
- *My World in the Literacy Hour – Wordworld* – Here you get literacy activities for KS1 grouped according to year and term.

Key Stage 2 materials

- Granada Writer/Textease (Studio) is an ideal word processor for this age range and IWB use as you can move text around the screen without restriction, and you can also draw next to text. It offers good versatility in the key mode of selecting and dragging, which is the most interactive important feature when using an IWB. Textease will work on any board, and with its built-in interactivity it is a must for IWB users.
- A teacher could easily use PowerPoint to create displays and talking books that would stimulate the children, but the slide shows are linear and text can't be moved around in an ad hoc manner. There is, however, a pen tool that allows you to write on a screen, but this does not compare with the pen tools found on an IWB. You would also need to spend some time becoming a good PowerPoint user to create appealing interactive displays. Textease has recently brought out a version similar to PowerPoint designed for children to use.
- There are many versions of word processors which will display text that can be annotated over using a pen tool. Most common are Talking First Word from RM, Writer from Blackcat, Granada Writer and, of course, Word itself.
- Clicker4 is an innovative piece of software in that you have two screens to work on. The first is a grid of text, pictures or both. You click on a word and it is displayed on a writing screen. Words and sentences are also spoken. This piece of software lends itself to use on an IWB as Cricksoft (the software designers) has created hundreds of grids to cover activities in literacy lessons. They range from letter recognition, nursery rhymes and phonic work to talking books. The grids available also cover KS2 work as everything is customisable when creating a grid.
- Sherston produce a whole range of CD-ROMs that seem ideal for use on an IWB and support literacy at KS2. Here are some titles:
  - Literacy Bank Y3, 4, 5 and 6 – This CD-ROM covers work on the National Primary Strategy (NPS), including activities such as cloze, comprehension, questions, etc. You can do lots of short activities or basic activities in groups or as a whole class – ideal for whiteboard use. Worksheets are available as a follow-up. No installation is necessary.
  - *Spelling Show* – This CD-ROM helps children to learn spelling patterns. You have large on-screen explanations followed by activities and tests. You could use this CD-ROM for whole-class or group work. You have to listen to on-screen voices that can't be paused, but you can annotate over screens.

- *Punctuation Show* – This CD-ROM helps children to learn punctuation. You have large on-screen explanations followed by activities and tests. You could use this CD-ROM for whole-class or group work. You have to listen to on-screen voices that can't be paused, but you can annotate over screens.
- *Grammar Show* – This CD-ROM helps children to learn grammar. You have large on-screen explanations followed by activities and tests. You could use this CD-ROM for whole-class or group work. You have to listen to on-screen voices that can't be paused, but you can annotate over screens.
- *Rusty Dreamer* – This is a talking book for older children. It is suitable for KS2, with graphics that look dated but which the children love. Good for whole-class reading, and display and annotation on an IWB. You could also use this book to aid map work.
- *The Reading Zone* – This is an on-screen dictionary. It could be used to go through the NPS word lists. It has indexed words, allows for a two-field search and has an extensive picture dictionary. You could easily use this on an IWB either as a short whole-class activity or as a constructive group activity.

- *The Oxford Children's Encyclopaedia* will display well on an IWB, allowing for English reference work.
- *Text Detectives* is a CD-ROM that delivers literacy skills with non-fiction texts. It's very new on the market and looks to give a good range of differentiated activities for Years 3 to 4. Skills covered include skimming and scanning, paragraphing and reference skills.
- *Grammar* is a KS2 CD-ROM that has 200 literacy-linked activities that look useful for work on an IWB.
- Granada Learning has produced some CD-ROMs that look good on and work well with an IWB. Here are some titles for you to consider:
  - There is a set of five CD-ROMs of talking books called *Twisted Tales*, containing titles like *The Pardoner's Tale*, *The Wreckers* and *Brockley Jack*. The stories are at two levels, with video and worksheet follow-up related to text level work. They cost £20 each and are good value.
  - Another set of talking books is the *Wellington Square* series, which contain stories and numerous literacy activities that can be worked on an IWB.
  - *Young Writer's Workshop* is a visual CD-ROM resource that supports writing reports and newspaper articles, and lends itself to group work with Year 5 and Year 6 at an IWB and computer. It is also a good source of ideas to use on an IWB, although the screens and text are on the small side for whole-class display.
  - *Writing Focus* is an application that uses audio, word banks and various templates to support literacy work. Its role in supporting IWB work lends itself more readily to groups of children working at a board rather than whole-class work. The CD-ROM is good as a rich source of ideas on how to

adapt work for the IWB. It could also be used for writing and modelling work on an IWB, although some of the text may be too small. You would use the pictures and sound to help with work.

- *Cornerstones for Writing* ages 7–9 and 9–11 are two CD-ROMs that support text level work and that will work very well on an IWB as the displays fit a large screen very well, and the activities themselves break down into screens that suit whole-class display or collaborative group work at an IWB.
- There is a series of CD-ROMs called Primary Literacy 3, 4, 5 and 6 that contain interactive literacy ideas that would display well on an IWB.
- A great piece of software to help with brainstorming is an application called Kidspiration. Also excellent is the software from Smatboard, called Smart Ideas, which can link to files, images and sounds. Using these programs you and your children can create ideas in words and images and then categorise them. These pieces of software look ideal to use on an IWB. This first product is distributed by a company called Tag Learning. Details can be found by phone, fax or e-mail as listed below.
  Tel: 01474 357 350
  Fax: 01474 537 887
  E-mail: **sales@taglearning.com**
  Website: **www.taglearning.com**
- The resources provided by the DfES *Developing Early Writing* and *Grammar for Writing* contain useful CD-ROM resources and have copiable text extracts for inserting into a flipchart. There are also the Additional Literacy Support packs that can be scanned and used in your flipcharts or screens.
- RM (Research Materials) have developed a literacy application called Easiteach Literacy, which works just like IWB software and which is designed to allow you to drag and drop text, link it together, mix text and images and so on. This software will run on any board and is well worth a look. Looking at the RM website at **www.rm.com** will give you access to further information.
- There is also a CD-ROM called *Searchlights for Spelling* by Cambridge University Press for years 2–5, which allows the user to manipulate, highlight and write over spelling patterns. It is easy to use and incorporates the IWB features in the actual software. This CD would be a big time saver as all the patterns for each year group are pre-prepared.

Contacts

Textease – Softease Ltd
Market Place
Ashbourne
Derbyshire
DE6 IES
Tel: 01335 343421
Fax: 01335 343422
E-mail: **sales@softease.co.uk**
Website: **www.textease.com**

Clicker4
Crick Software Ltd
35 Charter Gate
Quarry Park Close
Moulton Park
Northampton
NN3 6QB
Tel: 01604 671691
Fax: 01604 671692
E-mail: **info@cricksoft.com**
Website: **www.cricksoft.com**

Sherston Software Ltd
Angel House
Sherston
Malmesbury
Wiltshire
SN16 OLH
Tel: 01666 843200
Fax: 01666 843216
E-mail: **sales@sherston.co.uk**
Website: **www.sherston.com**

Granada Learning Ltd (including Semerc for *My World*)
Granada Learning
Quay St
Manchester
M60 9EA
Tel: 0161 8272927
Fax: 0161 8272966
E-mail: **info@granada-learning.com**
Website: **www.granada-learning.com**

2Simple Software
304 Sentinel Square
Brent St
Hendon
London
NW4 2EL
Tel: 020 8203 1781
Fax: 020 8201 6370
Email: **sales@2simplesoftware.com**
Website: **www.2simplesoftware.com**

I appreciate that there will be other titles that will be suitable for use on an IWB, but for the purposes of this book I have concentrated on the software listed to give a tight focus on resources for literacy and IWB use.

I would welcome suggestions for other software with open arms and can be contacted at: **l.j.sietniekas@hull.ac.uk**

IWB and the Internet

It can be very powerful to use an IWB in conjunction with the Internet. Here are some sites that you may find useful.

- **http://www.puzzlemaker.com** – This is a site that allows you to create puzzles, such as wordsearches, that you can save and then display on an IWB. It's easy to use and has good potential.
- **http://www.halfbakedsoftware.com** – Hot Potatoes is available as a free download from the Internet. Under their copyright laws you are allowed to create drag-and-drop-type exercises for your own use and to share via the web, but not for profit. These would certainly make your screens more interactive.
- **http://www.teem.org.uk** – This site gives you evaluations of selected CD-ROM titles which are very useful in deciding whether you wish to use them with an IWB.
- **http://besd.becta.org.uk** – This is a database of software to use across all key stages and is useful in finding resources that will supplement and support literacy lessons.
- **http://www.kented.org.uk/ngfl/websites/junior.html#english** – This section of the Kented website leads you to literacy sites that will support your use of the IWB in the literacy lessons, but it's up to you to pick what you want.
- **http://www.cricksoft.com/cgfl/uk** – This section of the CrickSoft site shows you what you can download into Clicker4 to use on an IWB in support of literacy lessons. This is free as long as you have a copy of Clicker4 and you register yourself on the site.
- **http://www.dialsolutions.com/mwol/register.htm** – This is the registration page for giving you access to downloadable *My World* screens for you to use on an IWB. You have to pay an annual fee for this service.
- **http://curriculum.becta.org.uk/literacy/index.html** – This site has the title of *Literacy Time* and has a whole host of KS1 and KS2 activities to review and then assess for use on an IWB. There are many texts that you can bring up and display and annotate via the use of an IWB. This site could prove invaluable to teachers as it gives lesson ideas that can be converted very easily for use with an IWB.
- **http://www.storiesfromtheweb.org/** – This has lots of stories for you to read and annotate online. You capture story extracts into a flipchart or notebook page to use with your class. This site caters for readers aged 8 upwards.
- **http://kotn.ntu.ac.uk/** – Kids on the Net is a site that offers access to written texts by children that you can display on an IWB.
- If you need to search for literacy resources, then you ought to use **http://www.ajkids.com** or **http://www.yahooligans.com**. These are sites for children rather than adults.

- The BBC site on **http://www.bbc.co.uk/education/schools** is a useful source of literacy ideas. A broadband connection plus Flash Macromedia is a very useful resource to have running, as downloads could be slow on a dial in connection.
- **http://www.acs.ucalgary.ca/~dkbrown/index.html** – This looks useful as a children's literacy web guide.
- There are the Kent Naturegrid big books on **http://www.naturegrid.org.uk/infant/bigbook.html** These are suitable for KS1.
- There are story starts from the Learning Zone on **http://www.sutton.lincs.sch.uk/pages/zone/story/start.html**. This resource looks very useful for working on an IWB and for supporting story writing.
- The Ambleside website has lots of literacy activities for you to explore: **http://ambleweb.digitalbrain.com/ambleweb/ambleweb/index.htm.**
- There's some interesting work on the MAPE site on **http://www.mape.org.uk**. You log on to the main site, click on the 'kids' section and download an activity called 'Disclose'. The children have to fill in text by choosing letters.
- Another MAPE address is **http://www.mape.org.uk/startower/starpunc/index.htm**. This activity allows you to download text that needs its punctuation replacing.
- If you go to **http://www.learn.co.uk/glearning/primary/lessons/ks2/lesson1/intro.asp** you'll find lessons on persuasive writing in adverts.
- The Grid Club is another useful site and can be found on **http://www.gridclub.com**. Click on the 'look it up' icon and indulge in dictionary work. If you click on the 'have a go' tab you can study proverbs.
- If you want some humorous poems, then go to **http://www.gigglepoetry.com/poetryfun.cfm**.

This is by no means a complete list and I'm sure you'll have your favourites, but it's what I use in my own work and if I listed more it would be overwhelming – what you have been given above is a huge amount of resources in itself.

Remember, too much will put you off, so focus on a little less. If you want a good guide then the book called *Online English* by John Lancaster from Belair (Folens) will give you a wealth of websites to refer to in support of finding whiteboard material to display via the Internet. These include stories, myths and legends, book reviews, etc. It isn't too long and gives you lots of English connections to explore in creating and identifying resources for the IWB.

Conclusion

I hope you have found this book useful, and that it has given you some ideas on how to use the IWB to support your teaching in literacy lessons. The main body of the book has related to starting ideas paralleling those given in the NLS handbook itself and is, therefore, very specific to what is required of you. I haven't referenced every point as not all the points lend themselves to IWB use.

I have included a software list that I think will work for you, the teacher, in delivering literacy via an IWB, but please remember to choose only the resources that are relevant to you, and not to follow it slavishly as the complete cure for using an IWB. Also, remember that some of the CD-ROMs I have mentioned have some parts that are good for IWB use and others that may be a little less appropriate. We have to adopt a 'best fit' approach when evaluating what works.

I have also given you a list of websites that I think will enhance your use of an IWB, but again I ask you to use these with care and not to rely on them as a cure-all for your work.

When I first thought of writing an IWB reference manual paralleling the actual NLS handbook, I was daunted by the scale of the work it would require. However, my motivation stemmed from the fact that my colleagues would be able to benefit from the ideas contained within it. It would show how this new technology could enhance teaching and learning in literacy and not simply be a glitzier method of delivery. Used properly, I believe this tool can help transform our teaching, and motivate and stimulate our students so that learning can be seen as something to be enjoyed rather then endured.

Finally, I ask you not to see this book as gripping bedtime reading, but as a working tool for ideas and planning whenever it is required. Dip into it, hopefully get a little inspiration from it, and then use the ideas to support your literacy teaching. I haven't written the book as a cure-all, and please remember the ideas are starting points for you, not complete solutions.

To end, please remember these simple steps:

- Use the board to show things – CD-ROMs, videos or the Internet.
- Ask the children to participate as much as they can. Learn to take a step back and let the children control the board.
- Encourage the children to interact among themselves, using the IWB as a stimulus. IWBs in themselves are not interactive – its how they are used that counts.
- Make use of the software that's on the market. It's not always completely suitable, but it will save you lots of preparation time. It also saves you having to learn the IWB software in great detail.

- When you're ready, create your own pages or flipcharts and start to think how you can encourage interactivity. This can be through the use of multimedia (the use of sound and video) and the use of interactive software, but the real answer is to use the board as a medium to spark interactivity between the children. Get them to work cooperatively, using the board to construct their learning. When you get to this stage, you'll really appreciate the value an IWB can add to your professional lives.

Happy annotating

L.J. Sietniekas
IWB Trainer, teacher, ICT adviser, teacher trainer 'CASCADE', The University of Hull

Glossary

This glossary is relatively short because it is assumed that the reader will look at the glossary for Literacy in the National Literacy Strategy book. It contains explanations that a beginner to IWB use might find helpful.

Annotation	Using electronic ink to create freehand writing or drawings that will sit over other applications.
Applications	Software you can run on your computer and display on your whiteboard. Often call third-party software in a whiteboard context.
Callouts	Speech bubbles you can draw out (can be found in autoshapes in Word).
CD–ROM	A storage medium for software or files.
Curtain tool	A tool that allows you to reveal parts of a screen a little at a time.
Document camera	A tool that allows you to view objects, including text, on an IWB or screen via a data projector. (Uses video signals.)
Flipchart	The name given to the space where work is created on a Promethean board.
Highlighter tool	A tool that allows you to put highlighted colour over objects on screen.
IWB	An abbreviation of Interactive Whiteboard.
ICT	An abbreviation of Information and Communication Technology. It refers to the application of computer skills to the curriculum.
Internet	The hardware and telephone setup that connects computers across the world.
IT	An abbreviation of Information Technology. It refers to the skills needed to use computers and associated hardware.
Notebook file	The name given to the space where work is created and stored using SMART board software.
Pen tool	A tool that lets you write freehand on an IWB.
Promethean board	A brand of IWB whose board uses a pen and software accessed from a floating palette.
Rubber tool	A tool that erases annotations and reveals whiteout text.
Scanner	Hardware that copies documents or images into software on your computer.
Select tool	A tool that allows you to choose and move objects on an IWB.
SMART board	A brand of IWB whose board uses a mix of pen or finger to work its software. It has a windows-type interface.
Text	Printed text created and displayed on an IWB. It can't be rubbed out with a rubber tool.
Whiteout text	Text that has been written over with white electronic ink on a white background, rendering the text invisible. This can be revealed when rubbed out by the rubber tool.
www	World Wide Web or the documents that populate the Internet. Each page has its own address and is accessed via the Internet.